OUR FRAGILE PLANET

FOOD AND WATER:

Threats, Shortages and Solutions

Jenny Tesar

Series Editor:
Bernard S. Cayne

A Blackbirch Graphics Book

Facts On File
New York • Oxford

Facts On File, Inc.
460 Park Avenue South
New York, NY 10016
USA

Facts On File Limited
Collins Street
Oxford OX4 1XJ
United Kingdom

Library of Congress Cataloging-in-Publication Data
Tesar, Jenny E.
    Food and water: threats, shortages, and solutions.
    (Our fragile planet; 6/by Jenny Elizabeth Tesar; series editor, Bernard S. Cayne.)
    Includes bibliographical references and index.
    Summary: Discusses the vital importance of having an adequate supply of food and water and the efforts of pursuing this need through various forms of storage and farming methods.
    ISBN 0-8160-2495-2
    1. Water-supply—Juvenile literature. 2. Food supply—Juvenile literature. 3. Agriculture—Juvenile literature. 4. Water—Juvenile literature. 5. Food—Juvenile literature. [1. Food supply. 2. Water supply. 3. Agriculture.] I. Title. II. Series: Tesar, Jenny E. Our fragile planet; 6.
TD348.T4 1992
333.91—dc20   90-47190

A British CIP catalogue record for this book is available from the British Library

Facts On File books are available at special discounts when purchased in bulk quantities for businesses, associations, institutions or sales promotions. Please call our Special Sales Department in New York at 212/683-2244 (dial 800/322-8755 except in NY, AK, or HI) or in Oxford at 865/728399.

Design: Blackbirch Graphics, Inc.
Reproduction by MDR Graphics
Manufacturing by R.R. Donnelley

Printed and Manufactured in the United States of America.

10 9 8 7 6 5 4 3 2 1

This book is printed on acid-free paper.

CONTENTS

1

NECESSITIES OF LIFE

What are your favorite foods? Steamed bass with black bean sauce? Grape leaves stuffed with meat and rice? Lamb curry? A fried vegetable dish called bubble and squeak? Reindeer steak with baked potatoes? Goat cheese? Ravioli smothered in a tomato-basil sauce? Fresh-picked corn on the cob?

People's favorite foods depend on their heritage, where they live and the experiences they have had. What people actually eat, however, may be very different from what they would like to eat. Availability of foods, buying power, nutritional concerns—these are important factors in what is actually served at dinnertime. For instance, people who live in wealthier countries generally eat more meat than people in poorer lands do. Meat is comparatively expensive; many millions of people cannot afford to buy it. Many millions of people also do not have access to enough fresh fruits and vegetables, to milk or to other foods that help ensure a healthy, balanced diet.

A Balanced Diet

For good health, a diet must provide a proper balance of proteins, carbohydrates, fats, vitamins, minerals and water. These substances are essential for growth, energy and the proper functioning of body systems. If a person's diet does not

Opposite page:
The food that we eat depends mainly on availability, which is in turn dependent on location and climate. What is considered fit to eat depends on cultural values as well.

include sufficient amounts of all essential nutrients, health is damaged.

Health also is damaged if a person does not get enough to eat. The human body is a machine. As with an automobile engine, the body needs fuel to function. This fuel, or energy, comes from food. The amount of energy in food is measured in calories. Generally, the amount of calories that a person eats should equal the energy used by the body. If more calories are taken in than used, the person gains weight, storing the excess calories as fat. If fewer calories are taken in than used, the person loses weight. Weight loss usually results from the conversion of stored fat into energy.

People generally eat a wide range of foods. However, the bulk of people's diets comes from foods called staples. Staples are people's primary source of carbohydrates, which are the nutrients normally converted to energy. They also provide iron and B vitamins. Cereals are the most widely eaten staples. Cereals are the grains, or edible seeds, of plants of the grass family. Wheat, rice, corn, oats, millet, sorghum and barley are the major cereal crops. Root crops, such as potatoes and manioc (cassava), and other starchy foods, such as plantain and sago, are also important staples. Staples provide at least 70% of the energy consumed by people. Different societies depend on different staples. Corn is the principal staple in Mexico, rice in much of Asia and manioc in parts of Brazil.

Another important food group and carbohydrate source for most people is legumes. Legumes include peas, beans, lentils and peanuts, as well as clover, which is raised as food for domestic animals. Legumes are good sources of many vitamins and minerals, and they contain more protein than do most cereals and root crops.

Meat, fish, eggs, milk and cheese are excellent sources of protein. They also contain important vitamins and minerals. For example, milk is an excellent source of calcium.

Fruits and vegetables are important sources of vitamins and minerals. Carrots and other yellow-orange vegetables are excellent sources of vitamin A; citrus fruits and tomatoes provide plentiful amounts of vitamin C; and green leafy vegetables such as spinach, kale and watercress are excellent sources of A, B and E vitamins.

Hunger, Starvation and Malnutrition

If people do not consume enough calories for a prolonged period of time, they lose weight not only from loss of fat but from the breakdown of proteins. Their bodies become emaciated and weak. They become vulnerable to illness and disease. Even though the percentage of people suffering from undernourishment has declined in recent decades, the actual number of sufferers has grown. According to the Food and Agriculture Organization, an agency of the United Nations, an estimated 27% of the population in developing countries, or 460 million people, were undernourished in 1969–71. By 1983–85, the percentage of undernourished people in developing countries had fallen to 21%, but the actual number of affected people had risen to 512 million. Most of these people live in Africa and Asia, and the majority of them lives in rural areas.

If undernutrition is not treated, people will eventually die of starvation. In times of famine, when many people go hungry, mass starvation may result. Some famines are caused by natural events, such as droughts, pest infestations and epidemics of plant and animal diseases. Three times during the 1840s, a fungal disease called potato blight struck Ireland, destroying most of the crop. Potatoes were the staple crop of Ireland, supplying about 80% of the calories in many people's diets. Without this staple, people starved. An estimated 1.5 million people died. Another 1.5 million fled, emigrating to other countries.

Other famines are caused by human actions. In the Soviet Union during the 1930s, government efforts to force people onto collective farms resulted in famines that caused up to 5 million deaths. In 1943, war-induced famine caused more than 3 million deaths in northern China. In 1991, a combination of drought and wars threatened 30 million people in sub-Saharan Africa with famine, with the worst suffering in Ethiopia, Sudan and Mozambique.

OUR DAILY CALORIES	
Country	Calorie supply per capita
United States	3,666
Spain	3,543
Germany	3,514
Poland	3,451
Canada	3,447
Netherlands	3,354
France	3,310
Egypt	3,213
Finland	3,170
Mexico	3,135
Argentina	3,118
Algeria	2,726
Indonesia	2,670
Colombia	2,561
Philippines	2,255
Mali	2,181
Tanzania	2,151
Benin	2,145
Nigeria	2,039
Bangladesh	1,925
Haiti	1,911
Chad	1,852
Angola	1,725

Source: International Bank for Reconstruction and Development/ The World Bank.

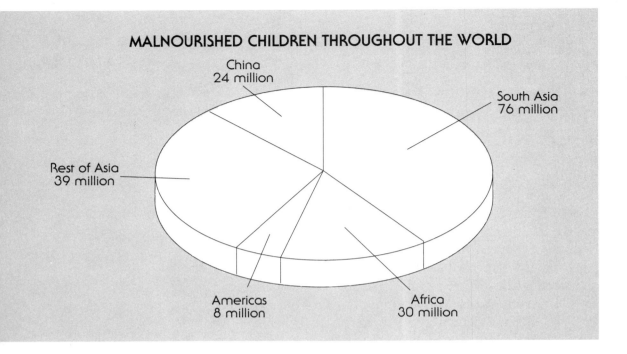

MALNOURISHED CHILDREN THROUGHOUT THE WORLD

China
24 million

South Asia
76 million

Rest of Asia
39 million

Americas
8 million

Africa
30 million

Undernutrition is a matter of quantity: people who suffer from hunger do not get enough to eat. In contrast, malnutrition is a matter of quality: malnourished people do not obtain the proper mix of nutrients needed for good health. Millions of poor people are overly dependent on staples because they cannot afford to buy the variety of food that makes up a balanced diet. As a result, they suffer from deficiency diseases. In parts of Africa, Latin America and Asia, for example, kwashiorkor is prevalent among poor people whose diets consist largely of plantains or manioc. Kwashiorkor is caused by a lack of protein. Muscles waste away, the skin swells with body fluids, the liver becomes enlarged and the person loses appetite and energy. Unless the person is put on a high-protein diet, death soon results.

Water: The Drink of Life

If you weigh 100 pounds (45 kilograms), about 70 pounds (32 kilograms) of you is plain, ordinary water. Every cell in your body contains water. Blood is 83% water. Muscles are 75% water. Even bone is 22% water.

Water is your body's most essential nutrient. You might be able to live for weeks without food. But you can survive only a few days without water. If the percentage of a person's body weight that is water falls by 5%, the person has difficulty in moving and in thinking clearly. If the percentage falls by more than 10%, the person dies.

Water performs numerous vital functions in your body. It is needed for digestion and other chemical changes. It carries dissolved foods and chemicals throughout the body. It lubricates organs and joints. It keeps the delicate tissues of the lungs moist, so that oxygen can be absorbed into the body. It removes wastes. It enables you to taste and smell.

Each day, an average person loses about 2.5 quarts (2.4 liters) of water through respiration and excretion. To remain healthy, this water must be replaced. Most people obtain about half of their daily water from liquids, such as water, milk and fruit juices. The remainder comes from foods, most of which contain large amounts of water. Lettuce is 95% water, cantaloupe 91%, green beans 90%, bananas 76%, ice cream 63%, pizza 48% and cheddar cheese 37%. Even meat is about one-half water, and bread is about one-third water.

The amount of water used per person is much, much greater than what we drink. Vast quantities of water are needed for agriculture, industrial processes and such personal activities as taking baths and washing clothes.

Insufficient water supplies pose a serious problem in many places. Fights and legal battles over water rights have erupted between communities, between farmers and city dwellers, even between countries. Pollution from sewage, industrial chemicals, pesticides, oil and other wastes created by people has contaminated large quantities of water. More than a billion people do not have access to safe drinking water. Each year, 4 million children under the age of five die from diarrheal diseases caused by polluted water and unsanitary living conditions.

Shortages Amid Plenty

Never before in the history of the Earth have harvests been so bountiful. In 1990, cereal production reached an all-time

> **COUNTING THE WORLD'S HUNGRY**
>
> An estimated 1 billion people suffer from hunger and malnutrition. How long would it take you to count the world's hungry people, assuming you counted one person per second? In a minute, you would count 60 people. In an hour, 60 times 60, or 3,600. In a day, 24 times 3,600, or 86,400. In a year, 365 times 86,400, or 31,536,000. In 31 years, 977,616,000. It would take you more than 31 years to count to 1 billion.

high of 1,784 million tons. Enough food was grown to provide every single person with the food needed for a healthy body and a healthy active life. Why, then, did some 60,000 people, including 40,000 children, die of hunger every day?

"Production is not the problem," said Guido de Marco, president of the United Nations' General Assembly, in 1990. "Distribution, transportation, storage and guaranteed access on a regular basis to suitable food—these are the principal obstacles which need to be overcome. These are the most urgent problems and should be treated as such."

Many people are too poor to afford adequate food. Governments do not give priority to improving agricultural production and distribution. As Oxfam America pointed out in 1990: "The amount spent on weapons every minute could feed 2,000 malnourished children for a year."

Poor farmers in developing countries cannot afford fertilizers and other purchases that might improve crop yields. They may be unfamiliar with good agricultural practices. Often they are forced onto poor-quality land that does not easily support agriculture. Overcultivation and overgrazing rapidly ruin the land, making it worthless.

Food and water problems are not limited to developing countries, however. Serious degradation and erosion of croplands and rangelands are occurring in most of the world's agricultural regions. Water reserves are emptying. Fishing catches are declining at some of the world's major fishing grounds. There is concern that much of today's plenty is enjoyed at the expense of future generations.

Soaring Populations

During people's first 2 million years on Earth, their total population probably never exceeded 10 million. Then, during the Stone Age about 10,000 years ago, people began to farm crops and domesticate animals. This provided more secure food supplies and the population began to increase. But by the year A.D. 1 there were still only 250 million people on Earth. It took until the year 1650 for that population to double to 500 million.

WORLD FOOD DAY

On October 16 each year, more than 140 nations observe World Food Day, an event sponsored jointly by the Food and Agriculture Organization of the United Nations, national governments and private groups. The purposes of the event are to make people more aware of the world food problem and to encourage them to work toward eliminating hunger and malnutrition.

Speaking at a special ceremony marking the observance of World Food Day in 1990, U.N. Secretary-General Javier Perez de Cuellar noted: "At the World Food Conference in 1974, the international community eloquently declared that every man, woman and child had the inalienable right to be free of hunger and malnutrition, in order to develop fully and maintain their physical and mental faculties. Governments solemnly pledged to eradicate hunger and malnutrition within a decade. Sixteen years later, we have more hungry people than ever before in human history....

"Time is not on our side. It is estimated that the world will have to feed an additional 1 billion people by the year 2000. The situation will surely become worse unless concerted efforts are made to address the root causes of hunger. Otherwise, millions of poor and disadvantaged people will be required to pay not only with their own lives, but also with those of their children."

During the 1700s and 1800s, there were many agricultural advances, leading to increases in food supplies. People's understanding of disease—its causes, how it is spread and how to treat it—grew. People lived longer. Babies who would once have died at birth or soon thereafter lived to become adults and to give birth to children of their own. Around the year 1830 the population reached 1 billion.

Rapid advances in conquering disease occurred during the 20th century, as scientists developed improved medical techniques and medicines such as antibiotics. Death rates declined dramatically, but birth rates did not go down in proportion. As a result, population soared. It reached 2 billion in 1930, 3 billion in 1960 and 4 billion around 1975. By 1991 there were more than 5.4 billion people on Earth.

Every second of every day, three more people are born. Every year, there are 90 million more people who need food, water, clothing, homes, medical supplies and facilities, schools, energy for heat and light, roads and other basic necessities. If so many people lack sufficient food and clean water today, what will happen when the world's population doubles?

The United Nations' projections indicate that world population will reach 6.25 billion by the end of the 1990s. By 2025 it will most likely be 8.5 billion. By 2050 it may well reach 10 billion. Nearly all the growth will occur in developing countries in Asia, Africa, Latin America and the Middle East. "By and large, the biggest increases will happen in the poorest countries; those by definition least equipped to meet the needs of the new arrivals and invest in their future," said Nafis Sadik, executive director of the U.N. Population Fund.

The largest relative increases will take place in Africa, according to the Population Fund: "By the end of the century, Africa will have 900 million people compared with 650 million [in 1991]. The annual rate of population growth will be 3%, the highest regional growth rate the world has ever seen."

At the same time that their populations have grown, most developing countries have experienced a decline in their ability to grow enough food for their people. The Population Fund points out that in 1969–71, developing countries imported 20 million tons of wheat, rice and other cereals. By 1983–85, cereal imports had risen to 69 million tons. By the end of the 1990s, they are projected to total 112 million tons. To meet these needs, other nations must have bountiful harvests. They must raise enough food to feed not only their own people but also needy people elsewhere in the world.

Meeting Future Needs

In 1798, British economist Thomas Malthus published *An Essay on the Principle of Population*. He warned that population growth would eventually outstrip food production. But Malthus had failed to predict technological change. He did not foresee the advances in crop productivity that have enabled farmers to grow more food than ever before.

Malthus's gloomy predictions have not come true. However, a significant number of people fear that the battle to feed humanity may still be lost. Among them is Norman Borlaug, the U.S. agronomist known as the father of the Green Revolution for his work in developing new wheat and rice strains that enormously increased crop yields and eradicated food shortages in many countries. "My interest in population comes through the kitchen door," he said in 1990. "Working on food, I began to think: Food for how many?"

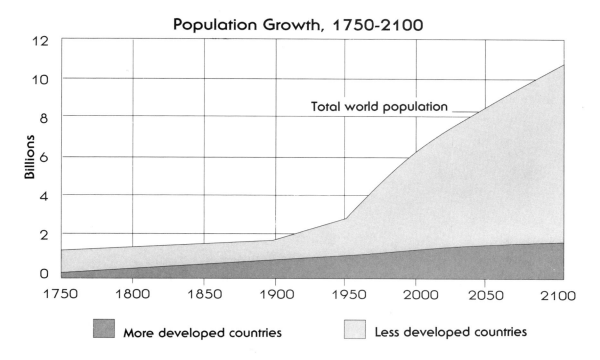

Population Growth, 1750-2100

Total world population

Billions

1750 1800 1850 1900 1950 2000 2050 2100

■ More developed countries   □ Less developed countries

Thomas R. Hargrove, a scientist at the International Rice Research Institute in the Philippines, noted: "By the year 2020 some 4.3 billion people . . . will depend on rice for most of their food. Global rice production must rise from today's 460 million tons to 760 million tons annually just to maintain current levels of nutrition, which are already inadequate."

Some people are optimistic that sufficient food supplies will be available, pointing to scientific and technological advances now under way. Geneticists are creating pest-resistant crops, cows that produce increased amounts of milk and other improved food sources. They envision corn that makes its own fertilizer, plants that can grow in salty water and fish that grow twice as fast and twice as big as typical members of their species. Soil scientists are working with farmers to maintain and improve soil quality. Water specialists are developing more efficient ways to bring safe water supplies to people, and to cleanse polluted water of its contaminants.

Will efforts such as these usher in a new Green Revolution? Will they eradicate hunger and thirst? Or will population growth render such advances inadequate?

2

SOURCES OF FOOD

People's foods come from three main sources: agriculture, animal husbandry and fishing. The earliest people depended on wild plants and animals for their food. They gathered berries, seeds, leaves and roots. They caught fish. They hunted birds, deer and other animals. But then, some 10,000 years ago—long before the start of recorded history—people began to raise crops. This intentional raising of useful plants is called agriculture. A dependable supply of food was the main purpose of agriculture. But plants were also raised to provide medicines, textile fibers, dyes and other products.

The Growth of Agriculture

As centuries passed, people developed many tools and methods to make farming easier and to increase the quantity and quality of crops. One method is selective breeding. People saved seeds from their most productive plants and used them to start the next crop; they discarded seeds from plants that had poor characteristics. During the 20th century, more sophisticated breeding methods have been developed, including gene transfer (see Chapter 6). Thanks to breeding methods, many different varieties of a particular crop now exist, each suited to certain needs or environmental conditions. For example, almost all grapes that are cultivated

Opposite page: Farmers in a small Asian village plant rice by hand in flooded fields exactly as it has been done for thousands of years. New technology that results in increased crops has not yet reached the small farms in most countries.

10,000 GRASSES

The most important group of food plants belongs to the grass family, Gramineae. Wheat, rice, maize (corn), oats, rye, barley, millet, sugarcane and sorghum are among the approximately 10,000 known kinds of grasses.

Grass seeds contain a large amount of stored food, primarily starch, which makes them an ideal food for humans and animals. The plants can be grown in a wide variety of soils and under very diverse climatic conditions. Rice grows in tropical and temperate conditions where it has a steady supply of water. Sorghum grows in dry, arid lands. Rye grows well on sandy soils in cool climates. Wheat adapts to many environmental conditions and is cultivated from the Arctic Circle to the tropics.

Wheat, rice and maize are the world's main staple crops. There are numerous species and varieties of each.

Grasses also are the main forage plants for cattle, sheep and other grazing animals. Grass withstands grazing better than most other plants because the leaves continue to grow from the base after they have been nibbled off at the top. Most forage consists of varieties that are not eaten by people, such as timothy, orchard grass and bluegrass. In addition, sorghum, maize and other varieties are raised as fodder crops. Livestock also are fed grain.

"All flesh is grass," reminds the Bible (Isaiah 40:6). That is, the grass eaten by domesticated animals contains nutrients that are used to build muscles (flesh, or meat). After the animals are slaughtered, their flesh is eaten by humans. Without grass, there would be no cattle or sheep—and no beefburgers or lamb chops for humans.

throughout the world are varieties of the single species *Vitis vinifera*. More than 5,000 varieties of grapes have been derived from this one species.

Another important technique is irrigation. Many areas do not receive enough water to grow crops. But if water can be supplied, either via pipes from rivers and lakes or by pumping it up from underground reserves, the land becomes arable. Irrigation has been practiced for thousands of years in countries such as China, India and Egypt. As early as 100 B.C. the Hohokam Indians irrigated fields of maize and beans in what is now Arizona. Today, about 15% of the world's cropland is irrigated.

Early farmers discovered that they could grow better crops if they added animal manure to the soil. The manure fertilized the soil, adding nitrogen and minerals that plants needed for growth. The farmers also learned that plowing ashes and crop remains into the soil enriched the soil. It wasn't until the 17th century that mineral fertilizers containing phosphorus and nitrogen began to be manufactured. The major advances in manufactured fertilizers occurred in the 20th century, after scientists discovered a method to make nitrates from nitrogen in the air. Nitrates are among the chemicals that plants need to grow well.

Over the centuries, people also developed ways to preserve food. Preservation protects food against spoilage, so that it can be stored for future use. The oldest preservation process is sun drying. It is still used for products from hay and grains to fruit and meats. One of the oldest preservatives is salt. Ancient peoples considered salt to be very precious. Part of a Roman soldier's pay was in salt. The modern English word *salary* comes from the Latin (Roman) *salarium*, meaning "salt money." Salting is still used to preserve certain foods, especially fish. Other methods of preservation include heating, freezing and irradiation.

As people traveled from one land to another, they took along precious seeds from their homelands. Indians from Mexico carried corn northward into what is today the United States. Europeans who explored North America obtained corn from Indians and carried it back to Europe. Then European settlers introduced wheat and barley to the Americas. In such a manner, the cultivation of specific crops spread across continents and around the world.

Progress in transportation also affected agriculture. Tractors and other machines meant that fewer people were needed to work the land. Trucks and trains could swiftly transport crops to processing centers and supermarkets in distant cities. Refrigerated vehicles permitted fresh foods to be transported even further from their source. The packaging of food became important, too; proper packaging can minimize spoilage, thereby extending the length of time that the food can be stored safely.

Today, farming practices are extremely diverse. Millions of people practice subsistence farming. They subsist on small plots of land, growing enough food for themselves but little or no extra to sell to other people. At the other extreme are huge corporation farms covering thousands of acres, where giant machines are used to sow and harvest crops. The range of farming methods practiced today is illustrated by slash-and-burn farms and modern high-tech farms.

Slash-and-Burn Farming

Slash-and-burn agriculture, or shifting cultivation, has been practiced since ancient times. Farmers would clear a small section of forest by setting fire to the trees and shrubs. The ashes from these plants would fertilize the soil, providing additional nutrients for the farmers' crops. Within a few years, however, the nutrients would be depleted. The farmers would abandon the field and clear another small section of the forest.

Over time, the abandoned field would slowly regenerate. Seeds from wild grasses, shrubs and trees would take root and grow. Eventually the forest would be restored. After several decades the area might once again be burned and used for crops.

Slash-and-burn agriculture supported small farming communities in tropical lands for thousands of years without seriously harming the environment. But as populations grew, farmers had to clear ever-larger areas of the forest. They had to return to abandoned fields before natural processes could rebuild the soil and plant life. This overuse of the land led to destruction of soil fertility and to extensive erosion. Some of the land became completely unusable. Neither crops nor forest plants would grow on it.

Today, slash-and-burn agriculture is still practiced in tropical lands. Vast tracts of rain forests are being destroyed to clear land for crops and livestock. In 1988, an estimated 12,350 square miles (31,987 square kilometers) of Brazilian rain forest were burned. The smoke was so thick in the city of Pôrto Velho that the city's airport had to be closed.

The widespread destruction of forests has many consequences. It destroys medicines, nuts, spices and other valuable products that can be harvested on a continuing basis from the forests. It causes the extinction of numerous plants and animals. It may even affect climate around the world. As rain forests are burned, the carbon stored within the trees combines with oxygen to form carbon dioxide. Billions of tons of carbon dioxide enter the atmosphere, increasing air temperatures and changing rain patterns.

High-Tech Farming

Traditionally, farms in the United States have been family enterprises. During the last decades of the 20th century, however, family farms have gradually disappeared. They have been replaced by immense corporation-owned farms. Agriculture has become agribusiness.

Mechanization plays a central role on large farms. High-capacity plows and cultivators, mechanical vegetable-harvesting machines, heavy-duty air-conditioned tractors and huge pneumatic conveyors are examples of the types of equipment used. Many processes are automated: computers control irrigation and the distribution of fertilizers and pesticides. Farmers use computers to communicate with data bases from which they get information on the price of supplies, disease outbreaks, weather forecasts and so on. The computers are also used to keep records on crop yields, milk production and farm finances.

Like slash-and-burn farming, however, high-tech agriculture can cause environmental damage. Modern agriculture is heavily dependent on irrigation, which uses up precious water reserves and can cause salts to accumulate in the soil. Synthetic fertilizers and pesticides contaminate drinking water supplies and harm wildlife. Machinery consumes large quantities of fuel, producing air pollution in the process.

Domesticated Animals

Like the origins of agriculture, the earliest domestication of animals occurred long before the dawn of recorded history. It is believed that sheep and goats were domesticated as early as 7000 B.C. and that cattle were domesticated around 4000 B.C. Animals were domesticated to serve as sources of meat, dairy products and hides. Some were domesticated to be work animals. Still others were domesticated for pets, hunting and sport. Indeed, dogs were probably the first animals to be domesticated, perhaps as long ago as 10,000 B.C.

The science of caring for, managing and improving domesticated animals is called animal husbandry. Among the

American pioneers in animal husbandry was George Washington, the first president of the United States. Washington had an experimental farm at his home, Mount Vernon, in Virginia. He was a leader in using new machinery, and he was the first person in the nation to breed mules. (A mule is the offspring of a male donkey and a female horse; almost all mules are sterile.)

Advances in raising animals have paralleled those in crop production. Breeding more productive varieties has wrought so many changes that today's domesticated animals show little resemblance to their wild ancestors. Farmers also have an ever-clearer understanding of animal nutrition and increased control over pests and animal diseases. As a result, modern milk cows yield much more milk than their ancestors did; sheep grow heavier, more uniform wool; and chickens lay many more eggs.

Animal-rearing practices vary widely. In parts of Asia and Africa, nomadic people move with their herds of cattle, sheep, camels or goats from place to place in search of pastures and water. In Australia and the American West, cattle and sheep roam over arid ranges covering thousands of square miles. In Great Britain and other lands with plentiful rain, herds of dairy cattle graze on lush fields of green grass.

Other livestock animals—including cows, pigs, chickens and turkeys—are raised in relatively small, confined areas. This practice is called factory farming. For example, calves raised for beef are often shipped to feedlots, where they are kept in enclosed areas and fed specially prepared feed containing high proportions of protein so that they will gain weight quickly. Some feedlots hold up to 100,000 animals.

Factory farming has been criticized for its heavy use of antibiotics, growth stimulants and other drugs. Cattle feedlots produce large amounts of excrement, which can contaminate water supplies. And many people are concerned that such intense confinement of animals is cruel and immoral.

Conventional rearing can also create environmental problems. The most serious problem has been the erosion of millions of acres of rangeland as a result of overgrazing.

In many countries, most cows, pigs and other farm animals are raised in confined areas. Calves raised for "milk-fed" veal spend their entire lives in small crates. They have no opportunity to be outdoors, exercise or even see other calves. They are fed a liquid diet that is low in iron. The animals become anemic. This retards muscle development, creating the pale, tender meat favored by consumers.

Chickens, too, are frequently confined. They live indoors in tiny cages, crammed so closely together that they cannot stretch their wings. As their bodies rub against one another, the friction can cause them to lose their feathers. To prevent the chickens from pecking one another, the tips of their beaks are removed.

In Sweden, regulations encourage the concept that farm animals should have as natural a life as possible. Dairy farmers are expected to allow their cows to graze outside at least part of the day. Pigs cannot be confined to cages and they are entitled to straw beds. Battery cages for chickens will be banned by 1999. And all farm animals must be fed a fully nutritious diet, thereby prohibiting the raising of sickly calves for "milk-fed" veal.

Another concern is the devotion of large amounts of cropland to production of alfalfa and other feed for grain-fed livestock. This consumes large quantities of water, energy, fertilizers and pesticides—plus acreage that many people believe could better be used to raise crops for humans.

Food from the Waters

Prehistoric people used their bare hands to gather clams and other shellfish from shallow waters. Later, they fashioned fishing spears and fishhooks. They made fishing lines and nets. They built boats. They learned how to use drying, smoking and salting to preserve fish.

As boats became bigger and bigger, fishermen were able to sail further into the oceans. Fishing grounds far from land were discovered and exploited.

Today, many fishermen still use methods very similar to those used by their ancestors. They use small boats and cast and haul in their nets by hand. At the other extreme are huge factory ships that accompany fleets of fishing boats. The factory ships are equipped with machinery to fillet, freeze and can the catch. Airplanes often accompany the fleets, to scan the surface waters for schools of fish. Echo sounders and sonar devices are used to locate fish swimming deep beneath the surface. High-intensity lights are lowered into the sea to attract fish, which are then sucked into a ship by powerful vacuum pumps.

By the late 1980s, the world's total annual catch of marine fish and shellfish had reached between 88 million and 105 million tons. These figures indicate commercial catches only. They do not include the tons of fish and shellfish caught each year by people for their own use or for local sale. Nor do they include the tons of freshwater fish and shellfish caught each year.

Almost half of the commercial catch is taken by Asian countries, principally Japan, which is the leading fishing nation. The Soviet Union is the second leading harvester of fish, followed by China, Peru, the United States and Chile. Hundreds of kinds of fish and shellfish are caught. The major portion of the commercial catch consists of relatively few species, however. Marine species such as cod, haddock, herring, salmon, halibut, sardines, tuna, mackerel, sole and flounder are the most important.

The negative aspects of advanced fishing technologies are apparent on some of the world's major fishing grounds. Many species are being harvested to the point where they cannot reproduce in sufficient numbers to maintain the population. Fish currently in danger of being overfished include haddock, halibut, cod, salmon and several kinds of tuna. For example, the number of large bluefin tuna in the western Atlantic—those age 10 or older, who are the major spawners—declined 73% between 1970 and 1990.

Modern techniques also take their toll on wildlife. Hundreds of thousands of dolphins, seals and other marine mammals are killed when they become entangled in fishing nets. Sea turtles are in danger of extinction at least in part because of shrimping activities. Studies have shown that shrimp nets killed more sea turtles in recent decades than all other human activity combined.

Aquaculture

For at least a few thousand years, people have raised fish and shellfish in controlled environments—a practice called fish farming or aquaculture. Artwork in an Egyptian tomb built some 4,000 years ago shows tilapia, an African food fish, being harvested from an artificial pond.

By 1990, fish farming accounted for approximately 15% of all fish harvested each year. More than half of this output occurs in Asia. China is the world leader, followed by Japan.

Some species are well suited to aquaculture. Carp, catfish and rainbow trout are important freshwater aquacultural products. Salmon ranches are growing in importance in marine waters around the world. Shellfish, particularly shrimp, oysters and mussels, are widely cultivated. Certain seaweeds are also cultivated, both for eating and as sources of chemicals used as flavoring and stabilizers in processed foods.

Aquaculture can be both a source and a victim of pollution. Fish wastes, including excrement and uneaten food, can nourish algae in the water. The algae grow rapidly and make the habitat unsuitable for the fish. Other concerns include the use of antibiotics and the possibility that diseases common to reared fish could spread to wild varieties.

Catfish are pulled from a large tank in the Mississippi Delta. Fish farming produces about 15% of all fish harvested each year around the world.

3

DISAPPEARING FARMLAND

 The Great Plains of North America have always been plagued by periods of drought. During these prolonged spells of dry weather, wild grasses survived. The plants' extensive root systems found moisture deep beneath the surface.

In the mid-1800s, farmers who settled in the Great Plains began to plow up vast expanses of wild grasses. They planted wheat and corn. These domesticated plants have comparatively shallow root systems and thus depend on a regular supply of water. After harvesting the crops, the farmers would let the fields lie fallow through the winter, exposing the soil to wind and water.

Beginning in 1931, severe drought descended on the Great Plains. Vast fields of wheat and corn soon withered and died. After a few years of watching their crops die, some farmers didn't even bother trying to raise crops. Nothing remained to protect the soil against erosion.

Strong winds blew across the land, lifting the exposed soil high into the air. Frightening dust storms called "black blizzards" darkened the sky and buried farm machines, buildings and railroad lines in dunes of dry soil. Some soil was carried as far as the East Coast of the United States, about 2,000 miles (3,219 kilometers) away. It polluted the air in Washington, D.C., and other cities, dirtied the snow on New England hills and even fell on ships at sea.

Opposite page: Erosion, flooding and misuse of the land are major causes of disappearing farmland around the world. Poor farming practices, irresponsible commercial developments and other human activities have greatly increased the loss of productive farmland.

The drought and its effects were most severe in the southern plains, which included portions of Kansas, Oklahoma, Texas, Colorado and New Mexico. This area became known as the Dust Bowl.

The damage caused by the drought and dust storms led to the establishment of the U.S. Soil Conservation Service (SCS) in 1935. This agency is responsible for conserving the nation's soil and water resources and putting these assets to good use. It now has about 3,000 local offices across the nation. Its staff includes soil scientists, soil conservationists, agronomists, biologists, geologists, engineers, landscape architects, environmental specialists, cartographers, recreation specialists and even archeologists.

Assistance provided by the SCS takes many forms. Demonstration projects show farmers and ranchers how to control soil erosion. On-site assistance is available for farmers and other people who wish to plan and carry out long-term conservation programs. Soil surveys describe the physical and chemical characteristics of the soils on more than 1.5 billion acres (.6 billion hectares)—about two-thirds of the nation's land area. SCS personnel can provide information about suitable crops for each kind of soil, help people control sources of water pollution and assist in the conservation and improvement of habitats for fish and wildlife.

Could another Dust Bowl form in the southern plains? Some people fear there is a strong possibility that this might happen. In 1952 and 1974, droughts again struck the area. They were shorter and less destructive than the drought of the 1930s. But they proved that the region remains vulnerable.

The Importance of Soil

Soil is one of our most precious resources. Without this thin surface layer of the Earth, farmers would be unable to plant the crops that compose the bulk of people's diets.

Hundreds of thousands of kinds of soil exist, each with its own mix of substances. Basically, however, soil is a mixture of nonliving particles, decaying organic matter and living things. The nonliving particles include sand, silt, clay and pebbles. The decaying organic matter, called humus, comes from plants and animals; it includes dead organisms, fallen leaves and body wastes from soil animals. Living organisms in the soil include bacteria, molds and other fungi, slugs, snails, centipedes, spiders, insects, worms, mice and moles.

Most soils consist of a series of layers. The uppermost layer, called topsoil, is the most fertile part of the soil. It has the highest amount of humus, which gives it a dark color. Soil organisms live in this layer.

Under the topsoil is subsoil. It contains very little organic matter and is lighter in color than topsoil. Animals seldom burrow down to this layer. Underlying the subsoil is rock. The freezing and thawing of water, plus other natural processes, break up the rock. In time, plant roots grow among the fragments and organic matter is added to form soil. This happens very slowly. It may take 30 years for one inch (2.5 centimeters) of topsoil to form from subsoil. It takes even longer for subsoil to form from the parent rock.

Properties of Soil

Soils differ in the proportion of sand, silt and clay that they contain. They differ in mineral content, too. Soil formed atop sandstone, for example, contains different proportions of minerals from soil formed from granite. The actions of organisms, the settling of dust and gases from the air and the movement of water also affect the chemistry of soil. For example, as water moves through soil, it leaches, or drains, certain minerals.

Certain elements are essential for plant growth. Three elements—carbon, oxygen and hydrogen—are taken mostly from air and water. The remainder must be absorbed from the soil. They include nitrogen, phosphorus, potassium, calcium, magnesium, manganese, sulfur, iron, zinc and boron. If these are lacking or present in insufficient amounts, plants will not grow well.

The amount of space among particles determines how much water and air can enter the soil. Water is needed by plants, which absorb the water through their roots. Oxygen from the air is needed by plant roots and organisms that live in the soil. Soils that contain a high percentage of clay tend to pack tightly, slowing the growth of plant roots. Very sandy soils may dry out because water quickly runs through these soils. The best soils have a lot of humus. They are crumbly, with lots of spaces into which air and water can enter easily. The humus also provides food for bacteria. Bacteria and other microscopic soil organisms feed on the particles of organic matter, breaking them down into substances that plants can absorb and use for growth. Among the most important soil organisms are earthworms. As the worms move through the soil, they leave behind burrows. The burrows break up the soil and permit air and water to enter. The worms help to mix the soil by bringing soil from lower levels to the surface. The worms' body wastes, as well as those of other soil organisms, contain nutrients that also enrich the soil.

SHIFTING SANDS

The Sahara of northern Africa is the world's largest desert. During the 1970s and 1980s, there were widespread reports that the Sahara was on the march, expanding southward into the semi arid region of the Sahel at a rate of 3.5 miles (5 kilometers) a year. In 1980, Compton J. Tucker of the U.S. National Aeronautics and Space Administration and other scientists began to collect data from meteorological satellites to verify these reports. They discovered that the Sahara was indeed on the march—but not always in the same direction.

Instruments aboard the satellites took daily measurements of vegetation along the Sahara-Sahel boundary. The data

showed that between 1980 and 1984 the Sahara expanded at a surprisingly rapid rate. Its boundary moved an average of 149 miles (240 kilometers) southward. Then, the trend reversed. In a single year, from 1984 to 1985, the boundary moved 68 miles (110 kilometers) northward. It moved further north in 1986, shifted southward in 1987, then northward again in 1988. In 1989 and 1990, it moved southward.

By the end of 1990, the southern border of the Sahara was 81 miles (130 kilometers) further south than in 1980. Tucker and his associates found evidence that variations in rainfall played a central role in the Sahara's movements. For

instance, they reported that rainfall in the Sahel region decreased progressively from 1980 to 1984, with 1984 being one of the driest years of the 20th century.

How critical are overgrazing and other land mismanagement? The scientists believe that data from additional years are needed before it will be possible to determine the effect of human activities on the Sahara's march.

Crop Yields

In general, the deeper the topsoil, the higher the crop yield. In one case, two fields that were side by side were planted with corn. One field had topsoil 12 inches (30 centimeters) deep; it yielded 64 bushels of corn per acre. The other field had topsoil 4 inches (10 centimeters) deep; it yielded only 38 bushels per acre.

Climate is an important factor in soil formation. In the tropics, soils tend to be rich in clay but poor in nutrients because frequent rains leach out nutrients. In temperate climates, grassland and prairie soils contain large amounts of humus and are very fertile. Desert soils have plentiful minerals but almost no topsoil because the lack of moisture limits plant growth. If deserts are irrigated, however, they can produce high crop yields.

Poor Farming Practices

According to the Food and Agriculture Organization, only about 11% of Earth's land area is suitable for agriculture. Each year, however, millions of acres of agricultural land become unproductive because of poor farming practices. The most serious problems are occurring in developing countries. But even wealthy nations such as the United States are experiencing significant losses of farmland.

Soil Erosion

Every year there are 90 million more people to feed—and 20 billion fewer tons of topsoil on which to grow food. The soil is eroded, or carried away, by water and wind. Erosion is a natural process, but farming and other human activities can greatly increase the rate at which it occurs. If fields are left bare during winter months in places where heavy rains and winds are common, large quantities of soil can be carried away. If hilly fields are plowed straight uphill and downhill, rainwater will run swiftly down the furrows. The running water washes away soil and forms channels that become progressively deeper until the fields are unusable because they are cut by gullies.

THE IDEAL WATER-USE SYSTEM

Trees and plants

Dam and powerhouse

In a perfect water-use system, human facilities work in harmony with natural forces to create an efficient and non-destructive cycle of usage. Trees and plants work to hold water on land and stem erosion and flooding. Reservoirs and dams create recreational areas as they store water for controlled release into hydroelectric generators. These generators produce power for waterworks and pumping stations that provide communities with water for various uses. Sewage from these communities is made harmless at a treatment plant before being returned to the river. Water from the river may also be used for irrigation of cropland.

Soil washed or blown from a field may fill irrigation ditches, making the ditches useless. It may be carried into rivers, where it destroys fish-spawning areas, blocks light needed by aquatic plants, fills reservoirs and causes difficulties for navigation. Rivers, in turn, carry soil to oceans, where it sinks to the bottom and is of no use to humans.

The loss of topsoil affects farmland in two ways. It removes nutrients needed by crops and it degrades physical properties of the soil, such as its ability to hold water for use by plants. Soil erosion also increases the costs of producing food. Farmers must compensate for lost nutrients with often-costly fertilizers. They must irrigate plants in soils that cannot retain water.

A 1990 report from the United Nations Environment Programme states that every year soil erosion robs Ethiopia of 1.5 million tons of grain. Soil degradation costs Canadian farmers $1 billion a year. In Australia six tons of topsoil are carried away for every ton of produce grown. In the Soviet Union, 2.5 billion tons of topsoil are lost a year; in India, six billion tons are lost.

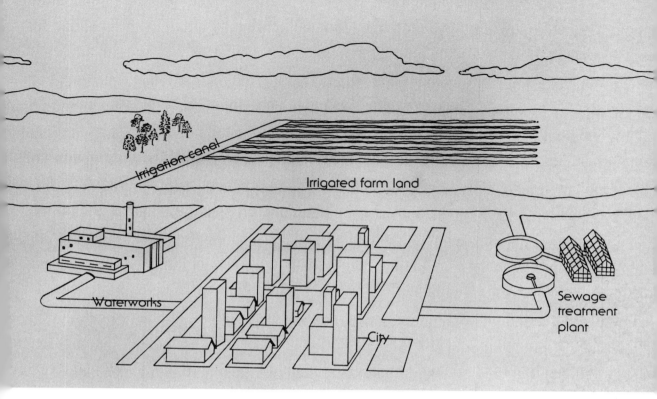

Irrigation canal

Irrigated farm land

Waterworks

City

Sewage treatment plant

According to data collected by the U.S. Soil Conservation Service, in the early 1980s water erosion on cultivated cropland in the United States averaged 4.82 tons per acre per year; wind erosion averaged 3.3 tons per acre per year. But soil erosion does not occur evenly; there is tremendous variation among farms. Two-thirds of the erosion on U.S. croplands in 1982 occurred on less than one-quarter of the land.

In arid and semiarid areas, erosion combined with drought may lead to desertification—the formation of desertlike conditions. Desertification is a problem in Africa, especially south of the Sahara, and in parts of northern China. In the United States, more than 225 million acres (911 million hectares) of land, mostly in the West, show signs of desertification.

Irrigation Problems

All water used for irrigation contains small amounts of dissolved salts. As the water is absorbed by plants or evaporates from the land, the salts remain in the soil. Over time, they tend to become concentrated—a problem called salinization. In areas with high evaporation rates, a thin deposit of salt may actually form on the surface of the soil. Salts, especially sodium chloride (table salt) and sodium bicarbonate are harmful to most crops and can turn once-productive fields into a wasteland.

When fields are overwatered, excess water may wash fertilizers, pesticides and other chemicals out of the soil. The chemicals enter water supplies, causing pollution that harms wildlife. In areas with poor drainage, overwatering may cause waterlogging: The soils receive more water than they can absorb or than can drain off. Like salinization, waterlogging hinders plant growth.

Salinization and waterlogging have reduced the productivity of millions of acres of farmland. They are causing particularly serious problems in India and Pakistan. In the United States, an estimated 25% of irrigated cropland has been harmed by salinization.

Worn-Out Soil

As plants grow, they remove nutrients from the soil. Under natural conditions, the plants eventually die and fall to the ground. Decay bacteria break down the plants' chemicals and return the nutrients to the soil. On many farms, however, crops are harvested and removed. Very little plant material is left behind to decay. With each successive harvest, fewer and fewer nutrients remain in the soil. Crops become smaller. Farmers say the soil has worn out.

Different crops remove different amounts of each essential nutrient. Thus worn-out soil is a particular problem on land that is used year after year for the same crops.

Monoculture

As plant breeders have developed more productive crop varieties, farmers have tended to switch from growing many different traditional varieties to growing a few high-yield varieties. In India, farmers once grew about 30,000 varieties of rice. Today, fewer than 10 varieties produce 75% of the

FOOD AND WATER
The Problems

Threats to our water supplies are also threats to our food supplies.

OUR FOOD COMES FROM THREE MAIN SOURCES: agriculture, animal husbandry and fishing. Each of these sources can be affected by various threats. Insect pests can destroy crops; viral diseases can rapidly kill millions of fish in fish ponds; drought can turn lush fields and grasslands into dust bowls. Natural forces create some of these problems. But human activities—such as overgrazing semi-arid lands, polluting water supplies and accidentally introducing insect pests into new lands—greatly exacerbate the effects of natural forces.

Far left: Drought-plagued corn dries in the afternoon sun.
Above: The Mediterranean fruit fly, or medfly.

Soil is one of our most precious resources. Each year, however, millions of acres of agricultural land become unproductive because of poor farming practices. Huge amounts of fertile soil are eroded from fields that are plowed incorrectly. Irrigation results in the build-up of salt deposits, which prevent the growth of many crops. Monoculture—growing a single crop variety year after year—removes essential nutrients from the soil, decreasing its fertility. The use of chemical pesticides destroys earthworms and other beneficial soil organisms. Often, the effects of poor farming practices are felt far beyond the edge of the fields. For example, soil eroded from the land is carried into rivers and streams, where it destroys fish-spawning areas, blocks light needed by aquatic plants for photosynthesis, fills reservoirs and interferes with ship navigation.

Herbicide is sprayed and incorporated into the soil on a farm in Kansas.

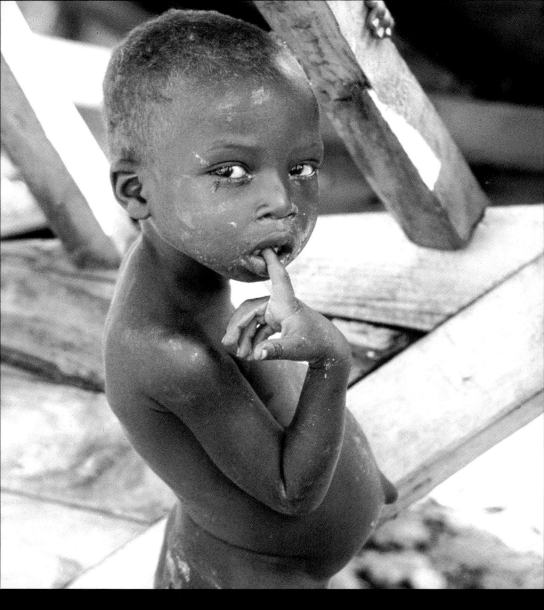

Above: A young boy suffers the effects of starvation in Haiti.
Far right: Eutrofication (stagnation) of water sources, which causes algae, encroaches on a rural lake.

EVERY YEAR, THERE ARE 90 MILLION MORE PEOPLE on our planet. In 1991, there were approximately 5.4 billion people on Earth. By the end of the decade world population will reach 6.25 billion. By 2025 population is expected to reach 8.5 billion. Many experts worry that it will not be possible to provide all these people with adequate food and water. Already, millions of people suffer from diseases caused by poor diets and polluted drinking water. Every day, some 60,000 people die of hunger.

MUCH OF TODAY'S BOUNTY IS ENJOYED at the expense of future generations. Inefficient irrigation methods and wasteful water use are removing water from aquifers much faster than it is being replaced by nature. Overfishing has led to declining catches at several of the world's major fishing grounds. Overcultivation and overgrazing are turning productive land into deserts.

A young Wisconsin girl frolics in the spray of a lawn sprinkler.

DISAPPEARING WETLANDS

Wetlands are swamps, marshes, estuaries and other areas that are regularly saturated by water. Some wetlands form inland and contain fresh water. Others lie along seacoasts and contain salt water.

Wetlands are extremely valuable. They provide homes for fish, birds and other wildlife. They serve as nursery and spawning grounds for many fish, including many species that are commercially important. During heavy rains, wetlands absorb excess runoff, thus helping to prevent flooding. Wetlands also improve water quality by filtering out nutrients, reducing sediment carried by floodwaters and breaking down organic wastes.

Until rather recently, people did not appreciate the value of wetlands. As a result, many wetlands have been destroyed. In the United States, more than half of the wetlands that existed in colonial times are gone. The major cause of this loss has been agricultural practices. Many wetlands have been drained and planted with crops. Others have been contaminated with pesticides and fertilizers.

In 1985, the U.S. Congress passed the Food Security Act, which included a provision that discouraged the conversion of wetlands to cropland. Farmers who planted crops on wetlands converted after 1985 became ineligible for certain government benefits. Tougher restrictions went into effect in late 1990. Today, farmers who convert wetlands to cropland are no longer eligible for all of the U.S. Department of Agriculture benefits to which the farmers would otherwise be entitled.

rice grown in India. In Sri Lanka, farmers grew 2,000 varieties of rice in 1959. Thirty years later, only five varieties accounted for most production. In the United States, half the wheat acreage is planted in nine varieties, more than half the soybean fields are planted in six varieties and three-quarters of the potato crop consists of only four varieties.

The growth of a single crop variety—a practice called monoculture—can have devastating consequences. Large portions of the food supply become susceptible to damage from pests or disease. The famine that caused the deaths of some 1.5 million people in Ireland after a fungal blight struck that country's vast potato crop in the 1840s is an example of what can happen. More recently, in 1969 and 1970, corn leaf blight destroyed more than 15% of the U.S. farm crop. Damages could have been far worse had not geneticists been able to quickly develop and distribute seeds that were resistant to the blight. In 1984, a bacterial disease called citrus canker was found in several Florida nurseries. The government banned the shipment of all citrus fruit from the state until each grove or grower was cleared. Some 18 million citrus trees and seedlings were destroyed before the outbreak was eradicated.

Troubles on the Range

Large portions of land are unsuitable for crop production but can be used to raise grazing animals. Covered predominantly by grasses, this rangeland is uncultivated and usually not irrigated, fertilized or seeded. For rangeland to remain healthy, its grasses must be allowed to regrow new, long blades before grazing animals return to feed. Otherwise, the grass plants die and the range becomes bare. Once the plant cover is destroyed, rain and wind cause erosion. Wherever cattle come to creeks to drink, or to cross them, they weaken or destroy the creek banks. The resulting silt can destroy the eggs of fish that live in the creeks and can even destroy the creeks themselves. This has been a serious problem in the western United States and in Australia.

In many places, rangeland is overstocked; too many animals are allowed to graze on the land. Grass is not given a chance to recover. In addition, compaction of the soil from the trampling of thousands of hooves degrades the soil to the point where plants are unable to survive.

Overgrazing by cattle and other livestock is a serious cause of soil erosion. In the western United States, 24% of the rangeland managed by the U.S. Forest Service is reported to be in declining condition or overstocked. Desertification caused by overgrazing is a problem in many countries but especially in Africa, where poor farmers and herders are forced to push their livestock onto marginal lands that already suffer from soil degradation.

Pollution

Food supplies are threatened not only by poor farming practices but also by forces outside farmers' control. Among the most serious of these forces is pollution.

Ozone pollution occurs when sunlight causes a reaction between compounds emitted primarily by motor vehicles and factories that burn fossil fuels. The higher the temperature, the greater the formation of ozone, in part because evaporation of chemicals speeds up in the heat. Chronic exposure to ozone slows the growth of many plants and kills seedlings. In southern California, which suffers from high levels of ozone pollution, the problem has caused reduced yields of many of the area's most valuable crops.

Acid rain is caused by the burning of fossil fuels, particularly coal and oil. Sulfur dioxide and nitrogen oxides are produced during the burning process. In the atmosphere, these gases combine with oxygen and moisture to form solutions of sulfuric acid and nitric acid. When rain falls, it carries the acids to the ground. As the acids seep into the ground, they can change the chemistry of the soil. They may deplete the soil of calcium and magnesium needed by plants. They also make the soil more acidic, which causes stress for many plants. In bodies of fresh water, increasing acidity has resulted in the disappearance of numerous fish.

Many scientists are concerned that global warming will pose a threat to food supplies in the coming decades. They believe that Earth's temperatures are rising because of increasing atmospheric concentrations of heat-trapping gases such as carbon dioxide and methane. These gases are formed during myriad human activities, particularly those involving the burning of fossil fuels. The scientists predict that the average temperature of Earth will rise by 3° to 8° F (1.7° to 4.4° C) by the year 2050. A rise of this magnitude will affect climate and weather patterns. Vast grain-growing regions in the Soviet Union and the American Midwest are expected to experience higher temperatures and less precipitation, which could transform these lands into semiarid grasslands or even deserts.

A Sense of Urgency

"From past generations we have already inherited a surfeit of denuded land and manmade desert which will never again yield food and in our times, as well, man's destruction of the world's natural resources has increased at an appalling rate. Unless this trend is reversed, we shall not survive." Edouard Saouma, director-general of the Food and Agriculture Organization, made these comments in 1990. His sense of urgency is shared by many people around the world.

4

CONSERVING THE LAND

During the Middle Ages, farmers in Europe began to use a new system called three-field farming. They planted one field in wheat, barley or some other crop. The second field was planted with a legume, such as beans or peas. The third field was left unplanted, or fallow. At the end of the summer, the farmers harvested the crops. Then they plowed all three fields, turning the crop remains on the first two fields and the weeds on the fallow field into the soil.

The next year, the farmers rotated their crops. The first field was allowed to lie fallow, the second field was planted with wheat or some other crop and the third field was planted with legumes. During the third growing season, the crops were again rotated.

By rotating the crops over a three-year cycle, the farmers found that they were able to maintain high yields year after year. The soil in their fields did not become "worn out." Crop rotation is among the methods still used by farmers to help conserve their land and maintain the health of their soil. Today, most farmers use a two-cycle rotation. They rotate legumes with other crops.

All plants need nitrogen for growth. Though air consists of about 78% nitrogen, plants cannot utilize this gas; they can only use nitrogen-containing compounds found in soil. These

Opposite page:
Many agricultural methods help farmers to conserve land and maintain high yields on fertile soil. Contour plowing, terracing and crop rotation are three of the most effective methods of soil conservation. The contour plowing on this Pennsylvania farm creates a beautiful pattern on gently sloping hills.

37

compounds are created—"fixed"—by certain bacteria in the soil. Other nitrogen-fixing bacteria live in small swellings, or nodules, on the roots of legumes. The bacteria take nitrogen from air and convert it into usable compounds. So important are the bacteria that legume seeds are often inoculated with bacteria before planting.

Soil fertility is improved by plowing under the remains of legume crops after harvesting. This is commonly done when fodder crops such as clover and alfalfa are raised. The decaying legumes increase the nitrogen content of the soil without the use of commercial fertilizers.

Soil Conservation

To decrease erosion, farmers use a combination of practices that slow the flow of water, giving it time to soak into the ground. These practices not only conserve soil but they often improve the soil's structure and organic content, thus increasing crop productivity.

Terracing is an ancient conservation practice used on hillsides. A series of flat, horizontal fields is created on a hill. To stop runoff, the fields are separated by ridges or ditches, or sometimes both. The width of the terraces depends on the

BADGE OF MERIT

"Education is probably the most important means of achieving any goal," noted Wilson Scaling, former chief of the U.S. Soil Conservation Service (SCS). "Teaching our nation's youth about the ways farmers and ranchers deal with conservation issues while maintaining production on their land can help instill the stewardship ethic in these young people."

Among the many groups that involve young people in conservation matters is Boy Scouts of America. In order to qualify for advanced ranks within the Boy Scouts, a member must earn awards, called merit badges, in various subject areas. One such badge is the Soil and Water Conservation Merit Badge. To earn this badge, the member studies such subjects as soil composition and structure; results of mishandling land; conservation practices; water pollution; and what can be done to improve land, limit erosion and prevent pollution.

SCS employees often help Boy Scouts earn the Soil and Water Conservation Merit Badge. Dennis Gaster, a cartographer with the SCS, has worked with Boy Scouts since 1971. He teaches the Soil and Water Conservation Badge at Boy Scout summer camps in New Mexico. The scouts aren't the only ones who benefit: "Teaching soil and water conservation to scouts makes me more aware of my own job and what SCS is really trying to do," says Gaster.

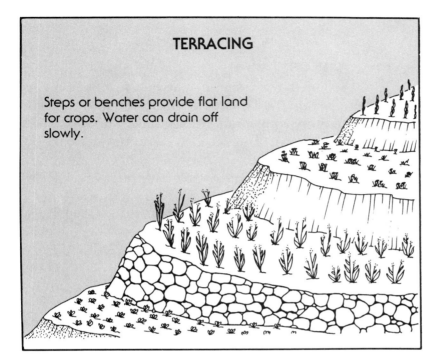

TERRACING

Steps or benches provide flat land for crops. Water can drain off slowly.

steepness of the slope, the amount of rainfall, the types of crops being grown and other factors. Narrower terraces are needed on steep slopes than on gentle slopes, for example.

A method used on gently sloping hills is contour plowing. Furrows are plowed horizontally with the contour—that is, around the hills rather than up and down. Strip cropping is often used with contour plowing. The farmer alternates strips of close-grown crops with strips of row crops. For example, soybeans may be alternated with corn. Rainwater running off the corn strips is slowed by the close-growing plants in the neighboring strips. As the water slows, it drops the soil particles it is carrying. The next year, the crops in the strips are rotated, helping to preserve the productive capacity of the soil.

Where wind erosion is a problem, shelter belts of trees are planted at the edges of fields. The trees slow down the wind. In winter, they trap blowing snow that can later melt and provide moisture during the spring planting season. In summer, they help cool the air, offsetting effects of heat and drought.

Conservation Tillage

The method used by a farmer to cultivate and plant land is called a tillage system. The systems that best prevent erosion leave one season's crop residue on the surface until the next season's crop is sown. This is called conservation tillage. In addition to limiting erosion, the residue maintains or improves soil quality. It increases water infiltration and reduces evaporation.

One common method of conservation tillage is mulch till. After harvesting, the field is plowed with disklike equipment that buries 30% to 70% of the crop residue. The rest of the residue remains on the surface.

The most effective conservation tillage method is no-till. The soil is not cultivated. Instead, the residue is left on the soil's surface. The next season, narrow slots are opened among the residue to sow seeds; no more than 10% of the surface is disturbed. No-till reduces erosion 90% or more. A study conducted by University of Tennessee scientists found that soil loss on soybean and sorghum fields using no-till was 98% lower than loss on similar fields using conventional tillage. Like mulch till, however, it is not suitable for all types of climates and soils. For instance, no-till may slow spring-time warming in cooler climates with wet soils, thereby delaying sowing and possibly lowering crop yields.

Sustainable Agriculture

Productivity increases brought about by new technology, better pesticides and improved fertilizers have been accompanied by increased production costs and environmental damage. Reducing dependency on high-tech inputs, in particular chemical pesticides and fertilizers, is part of sustainable agriculture—a practice that is also called low-input farming, organic farming and alternative agriculture. The objective is to sustain the productivity of the land without damaging the environment. Farmers who practice sustainable agriculture want their land to be as productive in the future as it is at present. They want to achieve this without poisoning water supplies, destroying wildlife and so on.

Soil conservation practices, from crop rotation to wise tillage, are a basic part of sustainable agriculture. For instance, by rotating carefully selected crops, farmers not only maintain soil fertility but they also disrupt the reproductive cycles of weeds, insects and other pests. This decreases the number of pests and, therefore, the need for chemical pesticides. Pests are also controlled by using natural predators, such as specific kinds of beneficial insects and birds.

Livestock and Rangeland

A new grazing concept that divides large pastures into a number of smaller paddocks eliminates the tendency of cattle to overgraze some areas and undergraze others. Cattle are kept in one paddock until they have eaten all the grass. Then they are moved to another paddock. They are not returned to the first paddock until the grass there has had a chance to

PADDOCK GRAZING

Paddock grazing is similar to crop rotation because it divides land into distinct units that are used in sequence. Cattle in one paddock clean an area thoroughly of all the grass. Then they are moved to another area while the previous area recovers.

IT'S THE LAW, BUT . . .

Often, governments pass good laws. Unless the laws are enforced, however, they are of little value. In the United States, the Bureau of Land Management (BLM), an agency in the Department of the Interior, is responsible for managing nearly 162 million acres (66 million hectares) of public rangelands in 16 western states. Its duties include monitoring vegetation and land conditions and overseeing grazing operations.

How effectively does the BLM perform these tasks? The U.S. General Accounting Office (GAO) examined the efforts of the BLM to prevent unauthorized livestock grazing on public rangelands. In a report issued at the end of 1990, the GAO wrote:

"An effective trespass enforcement program must offer reasonable assurance that offenders, especially willful ones, (1) will be detected and (2) when detected, will be assessed an appropriate penalty not only to penalize them but also to deter others from trespassing. BLM's trespass enforcement efforts do not meet either of these requirements."

The GAO noted that many grazing areas are inspected infrequently or not at all during the year. Ranchers who unlawfully allow their livestock to graze on public lands are not likely to be detected. When trespassers were detected, the BLM seldom imposed penalties. Many trespassers who committed serious violations were not even assessed the minimum fines required by law. "As a result," concluded the GAO, "grazing trespass is not adequately deterred, which can lead to degradation of public rangelands. . . ."

recover completely. The system also increases productivity. Don Proffitt of Pottersville, Missouri, says, "We used to run 50 cows and calves; now we're running about 75 most of the time on the same number of acres."

In countries where livestock is allowed to graze on publicly owned land, efforts to monitor grazing practices and environmental damage need to be improved. There also is a growing consensus that ranchers should pay higher fees for the use of public lands. According to a 1991 report from the U.S. General Accounting Office, fees paid by ranchers for use of lands managed by the Bureau of Land Management and the Forest Service do not cover the agencies' costs of managing the livestock program; millions of dollars of the costs must instead be paid by taxpayers.

Range Forage

Agricultural researchers continually try to find plants that will grow well under adverse conditions. For example, they discovered that a tall wheatgrass native to Russia grows well on saline soils. The plant, named alkar, has stiff stems and grows up to 6 feet (1.8 meters) in height. Alkar is now being used to control erosion and increase forage yields on ranches in the U.S. West. It also is being used as a wind barrier on farms.

An imported legume from Turkey has been welcomed by ranch managers in California and Alaska. Called lana woollypod vetch, it controls erosion; provides excellent forage for cattle, sheep and deer; and produces masses of seeds that are popular with pheasants, quail and mourning doves.

In western Kenya, the Food and Agriculture Organization introduced nine varieties of forage grasses and legumes that are highly nutritious, drought-tolerant and productive over a long growing season. More than 17,000 Kenyan farmers are feeding cows the improved fodder. Their milk output has increased an average of 70%.

Animal Wastes

In 1990, there were about 100 million cattle in the United States. They excreted 230,000 pounds (104,000 kilograms) of manure per second!

What happens to all this manure and to all the urine that also is excreted by the cattle? Much of it is simply dumped into the environment, where it causes extensive damage. Wastes from large dairy farms and cattle ranches at the northern end of Florida's Lake Okeechobee turned the lake's crystal-clear waters into dirty water laden with algae. The lake is a source of water for communities in southern Florida and for the Everglades. Several methods were used to decrease the water pollution. In some cases, irrigation systems were installed to enable farmers to use dairy wastewater on fodder crops. Streams were fenced off to prevent animals from lounging in the water on hot days. Cattle shades were built away from the streams, where the animals could keep cool and their wastes could be collected. The wastes could then be treated and spread on pastureland as a fertilizer.

"Feed lots" assemble large numbers of cattle or hogs to "finish," or fatten, them just before they are marketed. The high concentration of animals presents a serious problem of waste disposal. Some locations now prohibit such facilities unless the operator includes a plan for waste disposal.

5

USING CHEMICALS ON THE FARM

"It's a medfly!" The cry of alarm came in August 1989. Mediterranean fruit flies were discovered in Southern California. These flies had invaded the rich agricultural region before. In the early 1980s, California farmers lost $100 million in crops to the pest; government agencies spent an additional $100 million to eradicate the creatures.

Once again, the fight was on. The main weapon was the pesticide malathion, which was sprayed on infested areas from hovering helicopters. State officials maintained that the spraying was not harmful to people. But as the months passed and helicopters repeatedly sprayed communities, residents protested. Some people reported suffering from rashes, nausea and other ailments after each spraying. Parents worried about the long-term affects of the pesticide on their children's health. "We've been told too many times that things are safe, and found out later that they are not," said Patty Prickett, a Los Angeles parent who founded a protest organization, Residents Against Spraying and Pesticides.

Hundreds of damage claims and many lawsuits were filed against the state. Protest groups worked unsuccessfully to halt spraying. Sixteen months and $52 million after the first medfly was spotted, the threat seemed to be over—at least for the moment. How long would it be before more medflies

Opposite page:
The use of chemicals in agriculture has been controversial for many years. Many people are concerned about the long-range effects of pesticides and growth-enhancing chemicals. Others maintain that without these products food supplies would be in great danger.

entered California, brought in illegally on fruits or other plant matter? Would homes and yards again be doused with pesticide? Is there a better way to control medflies?

Indeed, there is a better way. Like all flies, the medfly passes through four stages in its life cycle: egg, larva, pupa and adult. The fly lays its eggs in a great variety of plants, including about 250 commercial crops. It favors plants with fleshy fruit, such as apples, peaches and citrus fruits. The eggs hatch into larva, which feed on the fruit. The fruit rots and falls from the trees. After a week or two of feeding, the larva leaves the fruit and burrows into the ground. It enters the resting pupal stage, during which it changes into an adult. When the adult fly emerges, it has one purpose: to reproduce.

Scientists have found a way to break the life cycle. They irradiate billions of medfly pupa with the radioactive isotope cobalt 60. The radiation makes the flies sterile. Vast quantities of sterile males are released into infested areas. Ideally, at least 100 sterile males are released for every wild female. The overwhelming number increases the odds that wild females will mate with the sterile males rather than with wild males. Female medflies mate only once. If they mate with sterile males, they will produce either defective eggs that won't hatch or no eggs at all. Using this technique, some medfly infestations can be kept under control without the use of malathion. But in 1989 in California, the outbreak was unusually large; not enough sterile males were available to eradicate the threat.

Chemical Pesticides

Medflies are just one of thousands of kinds of organisms that threaten food supplies. Other insects, viruses, bacteria, molds, weeds, blackbirds, rats and rabbits can cause enormous damage. Farmers use various methods to kill these pests or render them harmless. The most prominent method is the use of chemical pesticides. Pesticides include insecticides, to control insects; acaricides, to control mites and ticks; rodenticides, used against mice and other rodents; fungicides, to control mildews, molds, rusts and other fungi; and herbicides,

PLANT WARFARE

Many plant species have adaptations that protect the plants from being eaten by animals. For example, some species of wild potato plants have bristlelike structures called trichomes. Leafhoppers that land on these plants are likely to be spiked to death by the trichomes. If the invading insects survive this defense, the plants have a second weapon. They release a sticky substance that traps the leafhoppers. The substance quickly hardens. There is no escape for the leafhoppers—and no opportunity for them to eat the plants.

As scientists learn about plant defenses, they open up the possibility of applying their knowledge to improving agriculture. Some wild potatoes produce a chemical that, when released into the air, repels aphids. Cultivated varieties of potatoes do not produce this chemical, and they are susceptible to damaging attacks by aphids. If scientists could introduce the ability to produce the chemical into cultivated varieties, through cross-breeding and other genetic techniques, then crop yields would improve.

Some plants have weapons that are effective against other plants. Cucumbers release poisonous chemicals into the soil that inhibit the growth of mustard and millet, both considered weeds by farmers. If the chemicals could be synthesized in the laboratory, they could be produced and marketed in large quantities. Farmers could apply them as weed killers in areas where cucumbers are not grown.

to kill weeds. Pesticides are applied to seeds and soil before planting, on plants during the growing season and on harvested foods.

Agricultural use of chemical pesticides grew dramatically beginning in the 1940s, following the development of two poisons: DDT (dichlorodiphenyltrichloroethane) and nerve gas. These chemicals are typical of the two main kinds of synthetic pesticides. DDT is a chlorinated hydrocarbon, as are aldrin, dieldrin and chlordane. Nerve gases are organic phosphorus compounds; they include malathion and diazinon. Other kinds of pesticides include arsenic compounds, dinitro compounds and methyl carbamates.

Today, over 700 million pounds (318 million kilograms) of pesticides are used by U.S. farmers each year. Farmers say that chemical pesticides are essential if they are to maintain productivity and keep food prices low. But a study led by David Pimentel, an entomologist at Cornell University, found that food prices would increase less than 1% if U.S. farmers cut their use of chemical pesticides in half. Robert Metcalf, an entomologist at the University of Illinois, believes that Pimentel's estimates are conservative. He says that studies have shown that in some cases pesticide use can be reduced as much as 90% without decreasing yields or increasing food costs.

Undesirable Effects

Some pesticides are designed to harm only specific kinds of organisms. Others are broad-spectrum compounds. They kill many different kinds of organisms, including benign and useful organisms. For example, some pesticides are lethal to bees, which are needed to pollinate certain crops. Others kill earthworms, which keep soil crumbly and well aerated. Still others imperil insect-eating songbirds.

The volume of pesticides applied to a field is far, far greater than the amount that actually reaches the targeted pests. Most of the chemicals fall on plants or the ground and remain to contaminate soil and water supplies. Some are carried by winds to people and animals away from the farms. Many pesticides are not biodegradable. They do not quickly break down into harmless substances. Instead, they accumulate in the environment and in the bodies of living organisms. Among the most persistent pesticides are DDT and other chlorinated hydrocarbons. These pesticides can be passed through food chains, gradually building to toxic levels in birds and other wildlife.

Changes in the size of osprey populations along the Atlantic coast of North America illustrate the effects of DDT. Beginning in the 1950s, ospreys in the area absorbed large amounts of DDT through the fish they ate. The greater the amount of contaminated fish a bird ate, the higher the level of DDT in its body. Eventually, there was enough DDT in a bird's body to interfere with its ability to use calcium—a mineral needed for making egg shells. Female ospreys with high levels of DDT laid eggs with very thin shells, which were easily crushed by a nesting parent. From the 1950s to the early 1970s, the number of ospreys along the Atlantic coast fell sharply. Then in 1972, the U.S. government banned the use of DDT. Levels of DDT in the coastal waters began to decline. The osprey population slowly began to recover. In the 1990s, however, traces of DDT are still found in fish, birds and mammals and in sediments at the bottom of lakes, rivers and seas.

Even brief exposure to some pesticides poses risks to people's health. Each year, about 45,000 people in the

United States are poisoned to some degree by pesticides. Symptoms include headaches, vomiting, skin rashes, neurological disorders and, in about 50 cases annually, death. Some compounds have been shown to cause cancer, birth defects and miscarriages. The people most likely to be harmed are farmers, crop dusters and other workers who come in frequent contact with pesticides. For example, studies in several countries indicate that farmers exposed to the pesticide 2,4-D for at least 20 days per year have six times the normal risk of developing certain kinds of cancer. A 1990 report in a U.S. National Cancer Institute journal said that workers in flour mills have a cancer rate nine times that of the general population because of the workers' exposure to pesticides in grain storage.

Pesticide damage is economically costly. According to a study conducted by researchers at Cornell University, pesticide damage to the environment and public health, including human and animal poisonings, costs up to $4 billion a year in the United States alone.

The World Health Organization and national agencies set standards for exposure levels. Governments also establish the maximum amount of pesticide residue allowed in or on food. Standards vary greatly; some countries accept a higher level of pesticide residue in food than do other countries. Also, levels may not take into account differences within a population. For example, tolerance levels are frequently based on the amount of pesticide that an average adult can safely ingest. But some people, particularly young children and pregnant women, are believed to be much more vulnerable to harm.

MILK BOOSTER

Synthetic bST is a genetically engineered version of a natural cattle hormone, bovine somatotropin. It is nearly identical to the natural hormone, which controls milk production in dairy cows. When injected into cows, it raises the levels of bST in the cow's blood. This in turn causes the cow to produce more milk.

Supporters say that bST makes economic sense. They say that it boosts milk production in dairy cows by 10% to 25%. They say that its use poses no safety hazards to the cows or to people who drink the milk.

Critics say that bST does not make economic sense. They believe that bST's productivity claims are exaggerated. They say that cows who receive repeated injections suffer from reproductive problems and inflammation of the udder. They say bST's long-term effects are not known.

As with other animal drugs, bST is controversial. Many people question whether the potential benefits are worth the potential risks. As of mid-1991, use of bST in the United States was allowed only on an experimental basis.

Pest Resistance

When a pesticide is first used, it generally is very effective. It kills most of the targeted pests. But at least a few of the pests are likely to have a natural resistance to the pesticide. They survive and when they reproduce they pass on to their offspring the genes for this resistance. In time, there are so many resistant pests that the pesticide is no longer effective. Another, more toxic compound must be used.

Hundreds of pest species have developed resistance to one or more pesticides. Indeed, studies suggest that farmers who depend heavily on pesticides are fighting a losing battle. In 1945, U.S. farmers lost 3.5% of their corn crop to insects. By 1988, pesticide use was 1,000 times greater, and farmers lost 12% of their corn crop.

Alternatives to Chemical Pesticides

As pressure to make agriculture safer and less polluting increases, a growing number of farmers are decreasing their dependence on chemical pesticides. Many of these farmers follow a concept called integrated pest management (IPM). They use cultural, biological and chemical methods to control pests—with as little chemical use as possible. Instead of regular pesticide sprayings, the farmers monitor pest populations on their fields and spray only when the populations reach a certain level. Peanut farmers have reduced pesticide use up to 70% with this one simple change.

A common cultural method is crop rotation: alternating the crops grown on a field to help break the life cycles of pests.

Biological pesticides consist of natural compounds. An insecticide made from crushed oyster shells is being used to kill nematode worms that destroy the roots of vegetable crops. An insecticide containing toxins made by bacteria is used to battle the Colorado potato beetle. Insecticides containing sex attractants limit grape berry moths and pink cotton bollworms by interrupting their mating cycle so the pests cannot reproduce. Herbicides containing hormones literally make weeds grow themselves to death.

Introducing a pest's natural enemies is one of the oldest methods of biological control, and it often is very effective. Mites that feed on strawberry plants can be kept under control by predatory mites. Russian thistle, also called tumbleweed, can be controlled by a European white moth.

The future of biological pesticides appears bright, particularly as genetic engineers design microorganisms that fight specific pests and even design plants with their own built-in resistance to disease.

Chemical Fertilizers

Only if all the essential nutrients are present can plants grow in normal fashion. Three elements needed by plants are obtained from air, water or both; these are oxygen, hydrogen and carbon. The other essential elements are obtained from the soil. These include nitrogen, phosphorus, potassium, calcium, magnesium, sulfur and iron. If the soil does not contain sufficient amounts of these substances, fertilizers can be used. By adding nutrients to the soil, fertilizers ensure that plants have the chemicals they need for good growth.

Chemical fertilizers are widely used, and during the past few decades they have greatly increased world food production. "At a minimum, a billion and a half people are now fed with the additional food produced with chemical fertilizer," said Lester R. Brown, president of Worldwatch Institute.

Like chemical pesticides, however, chemical fertilizers can damage the environment. Farmers frequently apply excessive amounts of fertilizer to their fields. Much of the fertilizer is not used by crops. Not only is this a wasted expense but it may also injure or even kill crops. In addition, precipitation can carry the fertilizer into surface and groundwaters. In lakes, rivers and oceans the fertilizers can cause algae and other water plants to grow rapidly. The algal population may grow so rapidly that the water appears to turn green. As the algae die, they are decomposed by bacteria. More algae means more bacteria. The bacteria use up much of the oxygen dissolved in the water. Fish and other organisms cannot survive when oxygen levels fall too low. Fish kills—masses of dead fish lying belly-up on the water's surface—are often caused by explosive algal growth due to fertilizer runoff.

Farmers can limit their need for chemical fertilizers by adding organic matter such as cover crops, crop residue, compost and manure to the soil. Soil bacteria will decompose this matter, making the nutrients available for use by future crops. Crop rotation helps prevent the soil from being depleted of nutrients. And instead of planting crops on a flat field, farmers can use ridge tilling. In this system, crops are grown on small ridges separated by shallow rows. Fertilizers and pesticides are applied only to the ridges.

6

FOOD FOR
THE FUTURE

In 1944, the Rockefeller Foundation gave a young agronomist named Norman Borlaug a mission: Find a variety of wheat that will grow well in Mexico's soil so that Mexico does not have to depend on imported wheat. Borlaug tested many varieties of wheat. None had the necessary combination of characteristics. So Borlaug created new varieties.

Wheat is normally self-pollinating. The pollen produced by the male organ of a wheat flower is transferred to the female organ of the same flower. If the sperm cells formed from the pollen unite with egg cells in the female organ, seeds are produced. The seeds contain the same genes as those found in the single parent plant. Therefore, they grow into plants that resemble the parent.

Borlaug wanted to combine certain features of different varieties of wheat, so he forced cross-pollination. He removed the male organs from one variety and placed them in the flowers of another variety. The resulting seeds contained genes from both parents. They grew into hybrid plants—new varieties of wheat with some characteristics of both parent varieties.

Borlaug cross-pollinated Japanese dwarf wheat with very-high-yield winter wheat from North America. Then he cross-pollinated their offspring with various Mexican wheats.

Opposite page:
Scientific research includes creating new varieties of plants through cross-breeding and genetic engineering. These new varieties are produced to grow in areas where existing food plants cannot. The result is more land that can produce food for a growing population.

Finally, he created a number of high-yield wheats called Mexican dwarf varieties.

The new wheats revolutionized Mexican agriculture. Farmers who had produced 11 bushels of wheat per acre switched to the new varieties and got 39 bushels per acre. Within a decade, Mexico was producing enough wheat to meet its needs.

In 1963, Borlaug began to change his Mexican dwarf varieties to produce varieties that would do well in India and Pakistan. Soon, Indian farmers were tripling and quadrupling the amount of grain they harvested. Other researchers, inspired by Borlaug's work, developed new types of staple crops, including high-yield varieties of rice, corn, sorghum and millet.

The resulting growth in food production became known as the Green Revolution. The benefits it brought to a hungry world received special recognition when Borlaug was awarded the 1970 Nobel Peace Prize.

Another Green Revolution?

The work of Norman Borlaug was an example of selective breeding. Borlaug selected plants with desirable characteristics and crossbred them. Selective breeding of plants and animals has been practiced since the dawn of agriculture. It began when people saved seeds from their most productive plants, and when they decided which cattle, pigs and other domesticated animals would be parents.

In the 20th century, people learned that the characteristics of organisms are controlled by structures within their cells called genes. Genes control nutritional content of seeds, milk production of cows, flavor of tomatoes and size of fish. High egg production is another inherited trait passed on through genes. A hen that is a good egg layer can pass on this trait by contributing the genes for high egg production to its offspring. Similarly, wheat plants that grow well in arid environments are likely to produce seeds containing genes for this trait; the seeds will develop into plants that also grow well in arid places.

BACK TO THE FUTURE

Sometimes, the way to increase crop productivity is not to develop new methods but to return to methods used by peoples of the past. The Aymara Indians live on the floodplain of Lake Titicaca in Bolivia. For a long time, their crop yields were low. Frequent frosts killed many of their plants. Their potatoes rotted in the wet soil. Hunger and malnutrition were common.

Meanwhile, archeologists were studying the ruins of a successful Tiwanaku civilization that existed on the floodplain more than 1,000 years ago. Alan Kolata from the University of Chicago and Oswaldo Rivera from Bolivia's National Institute of Archeology were intrigued by a pattern of ridges and depressions on the floodplain. It reminded them of a pattern of raised fields separated by irrigation canals that had been reconstructed in areas where the Aztecs and Mayans once lived. Had the Tiwanakus used the same farming techniques at Lake Titicaca?

Kolata and Rivera set out to find an Aymara farmer who would be willing to experiment. Despite the opposition of his neighbors, Roberto Cruz dug canals and formed raised fields on his land. The effects were apparent at the end of the first year: Cruz's potato crop was seven times larger than the average yield of his neighbors.

By 1990, more than 1,000 farmers near Lake Titicaca were using raised fields. They even discovered an additional benefit to this technique: a free source of natural fertilizer. A thick ooze of bacteria, algae and other organic matter forms at the bottom of the canals. After the farmers harvest their crops they drain the canals and shovel the ooze onto their fields.

Until recently, breeders could only work with genetic material indirectly. Now, however, they can actually manipulate genes. They can transfer genes from one cell to another—a technique called genetic engineering. By inserting desirable genes from one species into another species, it is possible to develop improved varieties much faster than by using traditional crossbreeding methods.

Using a microscopic needle, scientists transferred the gene that regulates growth in rainbow trout into eggs of common carp. The eggs developed into "supercarp" that grew 20% to 40% bigger than their natural relatives. Tomato plants have been given artificially designed genes that made the plants resistant to a viral infection. Bacteria named *Pseudomonas fluorescens* have been genetically engineered to produce a toxic protein. Then the bacteria are killed. The dead bacteria can be sprayed on crops to control beetle and caterpillar pests. When the pests begin to eat the crops, the toxin quickly kills them.

Genetic engineering offers enormous potential. Someday soon it may be possible to transfer bacterial genes responsible for nitrogen-fixing into corn and other crops. Then the world could become less dependent on chemical fertilizers. It may be possible to create fish that withstand toxins that pollute rivers and oceans, plants that make their own pesticides and dairy cows that produce low-fat milk.

Some people worry that genetic engineering may pose risks. There is concern that introducing genetically engineered organisms into the environment might harm natural organisms and endanger food supplies. For example, if supercarp are released into the wild, might they cause the extinction of common carp? Might genetically engineered bacteria have unexpected harmful effects on soil, plants or even human beings? Might large-scale production of genetically engineered organisms further reduce the genetic diversity of crops and farm animals?

Few experts believe that genetic engineering is totally without risk. Government guidelines and laws are needed to regulate production of engineered organisms and their release into the environment. With care, however, genetic engineering might spur another Green Revolution.

New Attention to Underutilized Crops

Many foods of high potential value were long overlooked by agricultural scientists and researchers. Some of these foods were used only in small local areas. Others had been important to civilizations of the past, then were forgotten for one reason or another. Now these crops are being rediscovered and reintroduced to farmers. Agricultural researchers are working to develop varieties that are better suited to modern production techniques and to diverse environmental conditions.

One difficulty with introducing new foods is getting farmers and consumers to accept them. People are generally reluctant to change their habits. When potatoes were first brought to Europe from the Americas, Europeans thought they were "sinister." They believed the potatoes caused leprosy, syphilis and other diseases. More than 200 years passed before potatoes became an important part of Europeans' diets.

Three Promising Crops

Among the most promising field crops are the winged bean, amaranth and quinoa. All have the potential of becoming important staples in tropical areas.

The winged bean is native to Papua New Guinea. Its name refers to winglike rims on the seed pods. Before 1975, few people outside Southeast Asia had ever heard of winged beans. Then the U.S. National Academy of Science published a booklet titled "The Winged Bean: A High Protein Crop for the Tropics." Impressed by the plant's many desirable characteristics, farmers throughout the tropics eagerly accepted seeds. By 1982, winged beans were being raised in more than 70 countries. "Few crops have risen so quickly from total obscurity to the winged bean's current level of prominence," noted a 1982 report from the academy.

Except for the stem, every part of a winged bean plant can be eaten, which explains why some researchers call it "a supermarket on a stalk." The plant is an excellent source of protein; its tubers—enlarged roots—contain up to five times as much protein as potatoes. The leaves, which have up to 34% protein on a dry weight basis, also have high quantities of vitamin A, which is frequently lacking in tropical diets. Oil made from the seeds is rich in vitamin E. After the oil is removed, the remains can be turned into a protein-rich flour. The plants grow well in poor soils and are resistant to drought. Because they are legumes and have nodules of nitrogen-fixing bacteria on their roots, they do not require much fertilizer.

Five hundred years ago, one of the major food crops of Mexico's Aztecs was amaranth. Both the seeds and the leaves can be eaten. The seeds are rich in high-quality protein. Amaranth seeds have a protein content of 16%, which is more than that of wheat (12% to 14%), corn (9% to 10%) or rice (7% to 10%). Also, amaranth seeds contain the essential amino acid lysine, which is not found in wheat, corn or rice. The seeds can be ground into flour or cooked like rice. The broad green leaves taste somewhat like spinach but are a better source of nutrients; they contain large amounts of calcium, iron and vitamins A and C. Amaranth can be grown in a wide range of conditions, including semiarid regions that are subject to drought and soils that are somewhat salty.

A staple of the Incas of South America was the seeds of quinoa, a wild type of spinach. The seeds, which can be ground and made into pasta and flour, have up to twice as much protein as other commonly raised grains. They also are high in phosphorus, calcium, iron and vitamins B and E. Quinoa can be grown under a variety of conditions. In poor soil and drought conditions, farmers may get up to 1,700 pounds of seeds per acre (312 kilograms per hectare). In good soil and with adequate moisture, they may harvest more than twice this amount.

Insects as Food

In many countries, people eat a wide variety of insects. "In some modern, more developed nations such as Thailand, virtually everyone eats some type of insect," says Michael Burgett, an entomologist at Oregon State University. "You just buy them in the supermarket like milk and eggs."

Roasted giant waterbugs are a favorite snack in Thailand. Ant larvae are added to egg omelettes. Praying mantises are mashed into a paste. Silkworm pupae, a byproduct of the country's silk industry, also are eaten.

In Colombia, French-fried ants are sold by street vendors. Malaysians eat deep-fried grasshoppers. Cockroaches are an important part of the diet of Bushmen who live in Africa's Kalahari Desert. Honey ants are a favorite among Australian aborigines.

In all countries, insects are a frequent, unplanned part of people's diets. Weevils and other insects often infest flour, rice and dried pasta. Insects lurk in many fresh fruits and vegetables. Even processed foods contain insects. Government agencies sometimes set limits on how many insects can remain in processed foods. For example, peanut butter sold in the United States may not contain more than 30 insects or insect fragments per 3.5 ounces (98 grams).

Insects have two major advantages as a food. First, insects are an excellent source of protein. Pound for pound, termites contain twice as much protein as sirloin steak! Second, insects are very abundant and reproduce rapidly. Research projects that test the possibility of commercial insect farming are underway. They offer particular promise for those countries where eating insects is already an accepted practice.

Gene Banks

The Mexican bean weevil is a small, insignificant looking brown bug. But it causes great damage to beans that have been harvested and stored. Each year, it destroys as much as 25% of the beans stored in Africa and 15% of those stored in South America. Researchers at the International Center for Tropical Agriculture in Colombia spent five years trying to find a bean variety that the weevils would not eat. They tested approximately 10,000 kinds of beans, with no success. Then, a package of small wild beans from Mexico arrived at the center. When the scientists gave these beans to the weevils, the weevils wouldn't eat them. The beans were chemically analyzed; they were found to contain a protein that was not found in other beans. The gene that controls the production of this protein was inserted into other bean varieties. Now the newly resistant seeds are being planted by farmers in Africa and South America.

As farmers concentrate on raising comparatively few varieties of crops and animals, other varieties disappear and become extinct. Someday, however, plants and animals that have gone out of favor may be needed by people. They may have characteristics that make them better adapted to changing environmental conditions. Such is the case with the wild Mexican beans. Another example is a wild rice commonly called pig's weed that is in danger of extinction. At least one variety of pig's weed has a gene that makes the plants resistant to grassy stunt virus. Rice varieties commonly grown by Asian farmers are not resistant to this lethal virus. If there were to be an outbreak of the virus, scientists could try to extract the gene from pig's weed and insert it into other rice varieties.

To conserve genetic diversity, worldwide efforts are underway to collect and save the genetic material of as many

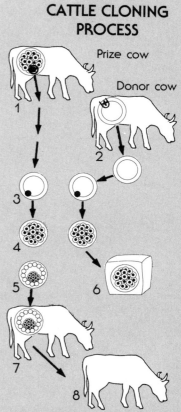

THE CATTLE CLONING PROCESS

Prize cow

Donor cow

Cloning begins with mating a prize bull and prize cow.
1. The resulting 32-cell embryo is removed from cow. Genetic material is extracted from several of the embryo cells.
2. Unfertilized eggs are taken from a donor cow. Genetic material in the nucleus of each egg is removed.
3. Genetic material from embryonic cells of prize cow is inserted in each of the altered unfertilized eggs.
4. Donor eggs and new genes develop into embryos.
5. Some are transplanted into surrogate mothers.
6. Others are frozen for later use.
7. After normal pregnancy, surrogate cows give birth to genetically identical calves.
8. Cloning process can be repeated using the same genes. Offspring are genetically identical to ancestors.

varieties and species as possible. For plants, this usually means saving seeds. Special seed banks have been established in more than 100 countries for storing seeds. One such bank is at the International Rice Research Institute in the Philippines; 86,000 varieties of rice from all over the world are stored there.

In most cases, seeds are cleaned, dried, bottled and chilled. Periodically, a small number of seeds from each variety are tested to make certain the seeds are viable—able to germinate and grow into mature plants. The U.S. Department of Agriculture's National Seed Storage Laboratory performs 20,000 to 25,000 germination tests annually!

Rare Animal Breeds

Like many plant varieties, numerous breeds of domesticated animals that once were popular are in danger of extinction. Conservationists are trying to locate and protect these breeds. Cooperative farmers keep herds of Dutch belted oxen, woodland white face sheep, mule-footed hogs and American cream horses. Organizations such as the American Minor Breeds Conservancy store frozen semen for rare breeds.

Various old breeds have proven to have valuable characteristics not found in today's widely raised animals. Finnish landrace sheep were near extinction in the 1960s when an animal breeder learned that the female sheep bear four or five lambs at a time. In contrast, commonly raised breeds bear only one or two lambs at a time. The Finnish landrace was crossbred with other varieties to increase the number of lambs per litter.

Navajo sheep were raised by the Navajo Indians for many years for their distinctive wool. Large numbers of the hardy sheep were killed when the U.S. Army declared war on the Navajos in the 1860s. Most of the remaining sheep were killed during the U.S. Navajo Livestock Reduction Program of the 1930s and 1940s; the government's stated aim was to reduce overgrazing and erosion on reservation land. In recent years, demand for the sheep's wool has led to a gradual resurgence of the breed. An estimated 500 Navajo sheep existed in 1985; by 1990 the population was about 1,000.

Stocks of wild fish are also important storehouses of genetic information. Some are threatened with extinction due to overfishing and to the development of hybrids by fish farmers. In Norway, which has one of the world's leading salmon farming industries, genetic diversity of salmon is preserved in a sperm bank.

Fish Farms

As overfishing depletes the supply of ocean fish, the potential contributions of aquaculture to the world supply become more critical. Increasing attention is being given by researchers to breeding, nutrition, disease control and other aspects of aquaculture. For example, researchers are trying to develop fish that can withstand low oxygen levels, which would enable farmers to raise more fish in less water. Growers of red abalone, a mollusk prized for its meat, found that they could make the abalone spawn more frequently by exposing them to ultraviolet light for several hours. Using this technique, the abalone spawn up to four times a year, in contrast to once a year for untreated animals.

FAO: WHAT IT IS, WHAT IT DOES

The Food and Agriculture Organization (FAO) is a specialized agency of the United Nations. Founded in 1945, it has a membership of some 160 countries. These countries have pledged to raise the levels of nutrition and standards of living of their people and to improve the production and distribution of food and agricultural products.

FAO is involved at every level of agricultural development. It provides technical advice and assistance to farmers, collects and analyzes information on every aspect of agriculture and advises governments on agricultural policy and planning. Some typical FAO projects are:

In the Niger, FAO has helped to plant 61,775 acres (25,000 hectares) of village woodlots and forest areas to protect watersheds, reduce wind erosion, fix sand dunes and provide renewable sources of energy. Of the more than 1 million trees planted in 1986, over a quarter were the fodder legume *Prosopis*, which thrives in poor soils and helps improve soil fertility.

Aided by an FAO project to introduce modern husbandry practices, farmers in Togo achieved a 50% decrease in lamb mortality within six years. They also achieved a dramatic increase in productivity as their female sheep gave birth to more lambs.

FAO's Global Information and Early Warning System on Food and Agriculture issues monthly reports on the world food situation. Special alerts identify countries threatened by food shortages.

Computerized databases coordinated by FAO contain information on every area of food and agriculture. For example, CARIS is a database that enables countries to exchange information on current research activities. The Remote Sensing Center helps member countries use images collected by satellites and aircraft to assess land, water, forest, grassland and marine resources.

7
WATER—A VITAL RESOURCE

An average person needs to take in about 2.5 quarts (2.4 liters) of water a day. Most people obtain about half this amount by drinking water and other liquids; the rest comes from the foods they eat. Vast quantities of water are pumped from wells and drawn from rivers and reservoirs to meet people's drinking needs. Even greater quantities are drawn to raise the food we eat. Worldwide, irrigation of crops accounts for about 70% of total water use. In the United States, irrigation accounts for more than 80% of all water used. In semiarid California, an estimated 170 gallons (644 liters) of water are used to raise 1 pound (.45 kilogram) of corn; about 2,000 gallons (7,570 liters) are needed to grow a pound of rice.

Industries require water for numerous processes. The major industrial use of water is for cooling. For example, water is needed to cool steam that has been used to drive generators in electrical power plants. Many manufacturing processes require large amounts of water. For example, close to 2,600 cubic yards (2,000 cubic meters) of water are needed to produce one ton of synthetic rubber; about 5,200 cubic yards (4,000 cubic meters) of water are used to separate one ton of nickel from its ore.

Water is also needed for personal use: to take showers, wash clothes, flush toilets, cook food, fill swimming pools, clean cars, water lawns and so on.

Opposite page:
Water, the world's most essential resource, is used in thousands of ways each day. Although human consumption and industrial use require vast quantities of water, irrigation of crops accounts for about 70% of the water used worldwide each year.

WHAT IS WATER?

Water is a compound composed of two elements: hydrogen and oxygen. Its chemical formula is H_2O. This means that a molecule of water is made of two atoms of hydrogen (H) and one atom of oxygen (O). A water molecule is the smallest particle that has all the properties of water.

Pure water is colorless, odorless and tasteless. But pure water is seldom if ever found in nature. Water is often called the universal solvent because it can dissolve so many different substances. As water flows over rocks, minerals in the rocks dissolve in the water. In the air, pollutants emitted from factory smokestacks dissolve in water vapor. People make extensive use of water as a solvent. Farmers dissolve fertilizers and pesticides in water. Manufacturers make soft drinks by dissolving flavoring and carbon dioxide gas in water. Doctors dissolve medications in water.

Water exists in three states in nature: solid (ice), liquid (water) and gas (water vapor). It moves among these three states in an endless chain of events called the water cycle, or hydrologic cycle. As the sun's heat warms the Earth's surface, it causes water on the surface to change to water vapor, in a process called evaporation. Plants give off water vapor from their leaves. People and animals give off water vapor when they exhale. The water vapor enters the atmosphere, where winds may carry it for great distances. As the vapor cools, it changes back into tiny water droplets, a process called condensation. Eventually, the droplets become big and heavy, and they fall to the Earth's surface as rain or some other form of precipitation. Some of the precipitation runs off into lakes, rivers and oceans. Some soaks into the ground. Some is absorbed by living things. Some evaporates and reenters the atmosphere.

As rivers flow toward oceans, they carry many dissolved salts and other substances that have been washed out of the land. These substances are dumped in the oceans. Because of the vastness of the oceans, a lot of evaporation occurs from their surfaces. As the water evaporates and escapes into the atmosphere, the dissolved substances are left behind. This increases the saltiness, or salinity, of the oceans. Ocean water and other water with high levels of dissolved salts are called salt water. Waters with low levels of dissolved salts are called fresh water.

The amount of water used per capita (by or for each person) varies greatly among nations. Sandra Postel, vice president for research at the Worldwatch Institute, reported that per capita use in 1980 in the United States was about 1,900 gallons (7,192 liters) per day. Usage in other countries was significantly lower: Canada, about 1,270 gallons (4,807 liters); Soviet Union, 950 gallons (3,596 liters); Japan, 687 gallons (2,600 liters); Poland, 343 gallons (1,298 liters); and Indonesia, 185 gallons (700 liters).

Fortunately, water is the most common substance on Earth. However, supplies are not unlimited. As world population grows, as the need for food to feed the growing population increases, and as developing countries become more industrialized, demands on water supplies increase.

Sources of Fresh Water

Water covers three-quarters of the Earth's surface—primarily in large oceans and seas, but also in rivers, lakes, ponds, bays, ditches and so on. Additional water is present in the atmosphere and in the ground. If all the water were spread evenly over the Earth's surface, it would form a layer nearly 9,840 feet (3,000 meters) thick.

Ninety-seven percent of all this water is salt water; only 3% is fresh water. Most of the 3% is frozen in polar ice caps and glaciers. Less than 1% of all the water on Earth is found in lakes, rivers and under the surface. It is this small, precious amount that most of the world's people depend on for their needs.

Fortunately, freshwater supplies are continually replenished by rain and snow. But the supplies are not distributed evenly, either in time or place. Some areas have wet seasons and dry seasons; during the wet seasons there is a lot of precipitation, but during the dry seasons there are extended periods of drought. Some areas, such as tropical rain forests, receive hundreds of inches of rain annually. In contrast, desert areas may receive only a few inches of rain a year. In the Valley of the Moon in Chile's Atacama Desert, it doesn't rain at all. Nothing lives there, not even insects.

Surface Water

Fresh water on Earth's surface is called surface water. It includes running water, such as rivers and streams, and standing water, such as lakes and ponds. When rain falls on land, some evaporates and some soaks into the soil. The rest runs downhill. It flows off the land into a body of water. The same thing happens with melted snow. The amount of runoff is affected by several factors. Some soils are comparatively porous, with a lot of space between soil particles. They soak up more water than denser soils do. Land covered with plants absorbs more water than barren land does. The seasons of the year also can affect runoff. There is more runoff during rainy seasons. In areas where snow falls, there is more runoff in the spring, when large amounts of snow are melting.

The land area that drains into a river or a system of rivers is called a watershed. Watersheds covered with trees and other plants regulate the amount of water that feeds into rivers. This helps to prevent flooding during periods of heavy precipitation and water shortages during dry seasons. Some watersheds are very small, covering only a few hundred acres. Other watersheds are enormous. The watershed of the Mississippi River stretches from the Appalachian Mountains to the Rocky Mountains. In addition to the Mississippi, this watershed is drained by rivers that eventually empty into the Mississippi, including the Missouri, Yellowstone, Platte, Arkansas, Canadian, Red, Ohio, Cumberland and Tennessee rivers.

Dams: Pros and Cons

Large amounts of water run downstream each year, entering oceans without having been used by people. But the flowing water of a river can be trapped, or impounded, by building a dam across the river. This causes water to back up on the upstream side of the dam. An artificial lake called a reservoir is created. The water stored in the reservoir can be supplied as needed to communities, farms and industries.

Most dams are constructed as multipurpose dams. That is, they are designed to serve several purposes. By controlling the flow of water, dams prevent flooding during periods of heavy rain and runoff. The stored water is then available later on, during the dry season, for drinking supplies, irrigation and other uses. The reservoirs can be used for boating, fishing and swimming. They provide refuge for birds and other wildlife. The water stored behind the dam can be moved through a hydroelectric plant. The water turns machines called turbines, which drive generators that produce electrical power.

Although dams provide important benefits, they also have drawbacks. Valuable farmland is often covered by the reservoirs. The system of dams built over the years by the Tennessee Valley Authority (TVA) to control floods and foster development in the Tennessee River Valley flooded 650,000 acres (263,000 hectares) of land. About half of this land had been used as cropland or pasture.

SNOW SURVEYS

In the western United States, snow is the primary source of the water supply. The snow falls in mountainous regions during winter, then gradually melts in spring and early summer to produce streamflow. It is important for farmers, power generators, fishery managers and other people to know how much snow has fallen and to know the water content of the snowpack. This allows them to estimate how much water will be available for their needs. Such information, for example, helps farmers to decide which crops to plant.

Since 1935, the U.S. Department of Agriculture has had a snow survey program. It has collected data on snow melt and estimated the amount of runoff from mountain watersheds. Originally, data was collected manually, by people who visited hundreds of sites several times during the course of a winter. Today, manual surveys have been supplemented by a highly automated system that can provide daily information on streamflow potential. This system is called SNOTEL (SNOwpack TELemetry).

A SNOTEL site has automatic measuring devices that determine the amount of water in a given volume of snow. This information is transmitted by a new technology called meteor burst communications. Very high frequency radio signals from the SNOTEL site are aimed skyward and bounced off the trails created by meteorites that enter the upper atmosphere. The signals are reflected back to Earth, to a master station. From there, the data is sent by cable to SNOTEL's central office in Portland, Oregon.

Construction often necessitates moving thousands of families from the area. About 70,000 residents were displaced by the TVA projects. The Aswan High Dam on the Nile River in Upper Egypt created a reservoir that averages 6 miles (9.7 kilometers) wide and extends 310 miles (500 kilometers) upstream. Some 100,000 Egyptians and Sudanese had to be resettled.

Tremendous amounts of water evaporate from reservoirs, particularly in warmer climates. For instance, the water that evaporates from the reservoir behind the Aswan High Dam equals about 25% of the flow of the Nile. Additional water is lost by seepage into the ground under the reservoir. Such losses greatly decrease the amount of water available for irrigation, power and other uses.

Another problem is siltation: the buildup of sediment in reservoirs. Running water erodes soil and other materials from the land. It carries these materials downstream. When the water slows down, it drops much of its load. A dam stops waterflow, and most of the sediment carried by the water settles to the floor of the reservoir. As more and more sediment is dumped, there is less and less room to store water.

THE EARTH'S WATER SUPPLY	
Salt water	97.2%
Ice caps and glaciers	2.2%
Ground water	0.6%
Lakes and streams	0.01%
Atmospheric water vapor	0.001%

For example, Glen Canyon Dam northeast of Grand Canyon National Park traps 87% of the 500,000 tons (453,600,000 kilograms) of sediment once carried by the Colorado River each day.

Dams change the ecology of a region, often affecting environmental conditions many hundreds of miles away. For instance, many farms are built on floodplains—areas that are periodically flooded by rivers. As the rivers flood the land, they deposit nutrient-rich silt carried from upstream regions. Dams prevent the seasonal flooding and natural fertilization of these lands, forcing farmers to use irrigation and chemical fertilizers. Following construction of the Aswan High Dam, the amount of silt carried by the Nile River to the eastern Mediterranean sharply decreased. As a result, the sardine fishing industry in the eastern Mediterranean was destroyed. The sardines had been dependent on algae, which had been dependent on silt nutrients carried to the sea by the Nile.

Water discharged from reservoirs behind certain types of dams comes from the bottom, where the water is coldest. This water can kill native organisms downstream that are adapted to warmer environments. Because the flow of water downstream from the dam is reduced and regulated, wetlands tend to dry up. In some northern California rivers with upstream dams, willow trees have begun to grow along the riverbanks. This has destroyed gravel beds where salmon spawned.

Salmon are among the fish that may be drastically harmed by dams. Salmon are born in cold northern streams. The young fish swim downstream to the ocean, where they live until they are several years old and sexually mature. Then they return to the exact same streams where they were born, to mate and produce a new generation.

Salmon cannot pass a dam unless fish ladders have been constructed around the dam. A fish ladder is a sloping waterway consisting of a steplike series of small pools. The salmon can easily swim from one pool up to the next one. At the top of the waterway, they enter the reservoir and continue to swim up to their home streams.

Another hazard awaits young salmon as they journey downstream. If the fish pass into a hydroelectric plant, they can be caught by the blades of turbines and stunned or hacked to death. This problem can be avoided by constructing bypasses that divert the young fish away from the turbines. Without bypasses, annual fish migrations are drastically reduced. For example, in 1990 the U.S. General Accounting Office reported that hydroelectric facilities in the Columbia River basin contributed to an estimated 80% decline in the annual migrations of salmon and steelhead trout.

Considering the pros and cons, it is not surprising that the construction of dams is often controversial. Among the projects that are currently the focus of much criticism is the plan to construct 30 major dams and more than 3,000 smaller dams along India's Narmada River and 41 of its tributaries. The Narmada flows westward from central India, emptying into a gulf of the Arabian Sea. To be completed around the year 2035, the project will provide drinking water and electricity for many millions of people and irrigation water for many millions of acres of land. But critics are concerned about the large number of people who will be displaced, including many from viable farmland that has been their home for generations. They point out that salinization of soils is likely to occur downstream from the dams. They also believe that silting will make many of the dams useless sooner than engineers predict. Many supporters of the Narmada project and other dam projects in India say they sympathize with the critics. But they say that these projects are essential if the country is to feed its people. In 1990, India had 853 million people. By 2025, the population is expected to be more than 1.4 billion.

Groundwater

When rain and snow fall to Earth, some of the moisture soaks into the ground, seeping into small, interconnected space between soil and rock particles. It moves downward until it reaches the water table. This is the level below which the soil is saturated with water. The water in this saturated area is called groundwater. In some places, the water table is at the surface. Here, water flows from the ground, forming a spring

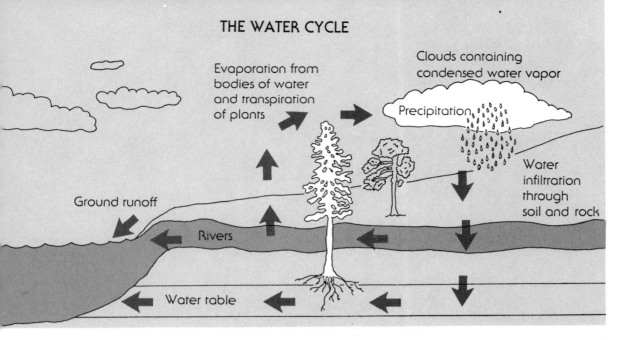

THE WATER CYCLE

Evaporation from bodies of water and transpiration of plants

Clouds containing condensed water vapor

Precipitation

Water infiltration through soil and rock

Ground runoff

Rivers

Water table

that feeds a lake, stream or wetland. Elsewhere, the water table is far beneath the surface.

Unlike the surface of rivers and lakes, the water table is not level. It is higher in some places than in others. Generally, a water table slopes downward toward a stream or ocean. It is higher in a mountain than under a neighboring valley—though it is probably much deeper beneath the surface of the mountaintop than beneath the surface of the valley.

A water-soaked region under the ground is called an aquifer. An aquifer can be thought of as an underground reservoir. Some people call the water in an aquifer "fossil water" because much of it has been stored there for hundreds of thousands of years.

To reach an aquifer, people dig or drill wells, then pump up the water. Precipitation and water from lakes and streams seep into the ground, replenishing the aquifer. But if groundwater is removed faster than it is replaced, the volume of water stored in the aquifer is reduced and the water table falls. Wells may run dry. They may have to be dug deeper to reach water.

In many parts of the world, groundwater resources are being rapidly drained. In recent years, for example, Saudi Arabia has used its groundwater supplies to greatly increase agricultural production. In 1984, Saudi farms produced 15%

of the country's food; by 1989, just five years later, production had jumped to 35%. U.S. experts predicted that all of Saudi Arabia's groundwater will be drained by early in the 21st century unless removal rates are drastically decreased.

As water is removed from an aquifer, there also is the danger of subsidence. The water helped to support overlying rock and soil. Without this support the ground sinks, or subsides. Mexico City, Houston, Tokyo and Venice are among urban areas that have experienced subsidence due to extraction of groundwater. Protecting or repairing roads, buildings and other property affected by subsidence is possible but expensive—particularly in cities. Subsidence may be gradual or sudden. In places where there are underground caverns, lowering of the water table may trigger the formation of large craters called sinkholes. This is a common occurrence in parts of Florida and Alabama.

Researchers are studying ways to refill, or recharge, depleted aquifers. In one experimental method, water is piped from rivers to holes drilled into the ground above the aquifer. In another method, water is sprayed over the ground surface so that it will seep down toward the aquifer. If such methods become practical, water that would otherwise be lost, such as floodwater, could be stored for future use.

The Ogallala

About half the U.S. population depends on groundwater sources for its domestic water. Groundwater is also used for about half the nation's agricultural irrigation and for nearly one-third its industrial water needs.

The largest U.S. aquifer is the Ogallala. This huge deposit of water-laden sand, silt and gravel extends from South Dakota southward to the Texas and New Mexico border. It covers about 170,000 square miles (440,300 square kilometers), and it contains about 3.3 billion acre-feet of water. One acre-foot, which covers one acre with one foot of water, equals 325,848 gallons (1,233,432 liters). This is enough water to cover all 50 U.S. states with a layer of water almost 1.5 feet (.46 meter) deep!

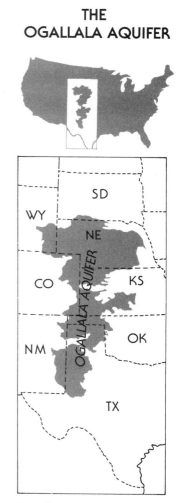

THE OGALLALA AQUIFER

The Ogallala, the largest aquifer in the United States, extends from the southern tip of South Dakota down as far as mid-Texas and covers regions in Wyoming, Nebraska, Colorado, Kansas, Oklahoma and New Mexico.

Millions of acres of U.S. farmland and rangeland are irrigated with water from the Ogallala. Up to 40% of the nation's beef and 25% of its food and fiber crops are produced on land irrigated with water from the Ogallala.

Water is being withdrawn from the Ogallala much faster than it is being replaced by nature. As a result, the aquifer is being rapidly drained and many wells have been pumped dry. In parts of the aquifer underlying Texas, water levels dropped 50 feet (15.2 meters) or more between 1940 and 1980. By 1990, experts estimated that 11% of the aquifer's water had been removed since the 1930s and that 25% of the water will be gone by 2020.

Another problem is contamination, primarily from agricultural wastes. In 1987, for example, farmers and ranchers in Nebraska used 775,000 tons (703,080,000 kilograms) of fertilizer, plus uncounted tons of pesticides. Their cows and hogs produced 235,000 tons (213,192,000 kilograms) of manure. It is easy for these materials to leach downward and pollute the aquifer.

Desalination

It is possible to separate seawater into two parts: pure water and a thick watery salt solution called brine. Extracting pure water out of seawater is called desalination or desalinization. The water can be used just like water from a river or aquifer. However, it lacks the minerals that give fresh water its pleasant taste, so the pure water is usually mixed with some fresh water to form drinking water.

There are thousands of desalination facilities around the world. They range from small household units to giant plants that produce enough water to supply entire cities. More than half of the world's desalted water is produced in the Persian Gulf countries of Saudi Arabia, Kuwait, the United Arab Emirates, Qatar and Bahrain. These arid lands depend on desalination for almost all their water supplies. Saudi Arabia has the world's most ambitious desalination program. Its plant at Jubail is the world's largest, able to produce 38.7 million cubic feet (1.1 million cubic meters) of water daily.

DESALINATION – DRINKING WATER FROM THE SEA BY REVERSE OSMOSIS

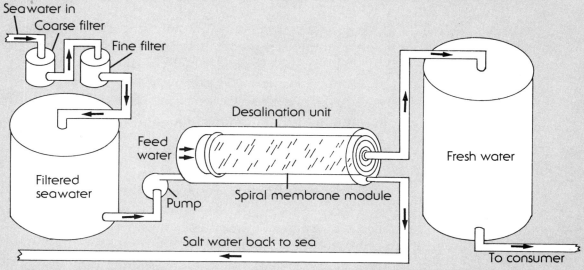

Seawater contains pure water, many kinds of undissolved particles and many dissolved substances, mostly salt. In a reverse-osmosis plant, the undissolved particles are removed first by passing the seawater through a series of filters. The water molecules are then separated from the molecules of dissolved substances by reverse osmosis. In the desalination unit, seawater is pumped under high pressure along a semipermeable membrane. Water molecules cross the membrane and are collected. About one gallon of fresh water is obtained from every three gallons of seawater that pass through the desalination unit. The salt dissolved in the remaining seawater is returned to the sea.

The number of desalination plants has increased steadily in recent years. This trend is expected to continue as freshwater supplies fail to meet the needs of growing populations. It is expensive to build and operate desalination plants, though costs have declined as more efficient processes and equipment have been developed. "You back into desalination," said a California engineer. "You do it when you don't have other choices."

Two basic concepts are used by modern desalination plants: distillation and membrane processes.

Distillation

The most widely used desalination process is multistage flash distillation. This process makes use of the fact that the temperature at which water boils depends on the pressure. Under normal pressure—that is, at sea level—water boils at 212°F (100°C). But if the pressure is lowered, the water will boil at a lower temperature. In a multistage flash distillation plant, seawater is heated to boiling or even higher, but it is not allowed to boil because of high pressure. Then the water is sent into a chamber where the pressure is low. This causes some of the water to flash, or boil instantly. The resulting steam rises. When the steam hits condensing coils carrying incoming seawater, it cools and condenses as pure water. The liquid droplets fall onto trays that empty into a collecting tank. The salty water that is left behind is called brine. It may be passed through as many as 60 flashing stages to extract as much pure water as possible. When the brine finally leaves the plant, it typically is discharged into the ocean.

Solar distillation is an ancient process that was used more than 2,000 years ago by Julius Caesar to obtain drinking water for his soldiers. He built solar evaporators to distill water from the Mediterranean Sea. Today's solar systems use large black basins called solar stills. The top of the basin has a sloping cover made of clear glass or plastic. When the sun shines through the cover onto seawater in the basin, it heats the

PLANTS FOR DAMAGED AND SALTY SOILS

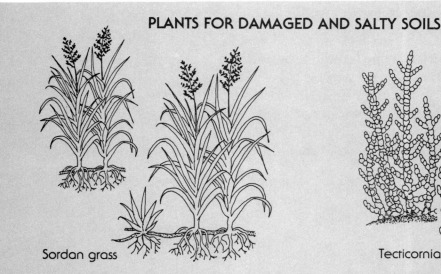

Sordan grass

This grass repairs soil made crusty by sodium compounds. The grass releases acids that dissolve calcium carbonate producing calcium and carbon dioxide. Calcium displaces sodium in the soil. The sodium dissolves and joins with carbon dioxide to form sodium bicarbonate, which washes away.

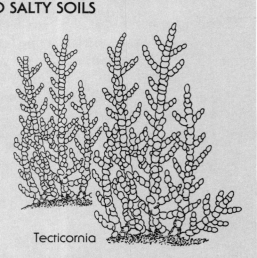

Tecticornia

A salt-tolerant plant that yields seeds. The Australian aborigines grind the seeds into a flour that can be used for bread. It grows in coastal mud flats above the normal tidal level.

water. Some of the water evaporates and the water vapor rises to the cover. When the water vapor hits the cool cover, it condenses, forming drops that trickle down the sloping cover to a collecting trough.

Membrane Processes

Pure water also can be obtained from salt water with processes that use a thin, semipermeable membrane. This is a membrane that is permeable to only some substances. That is, it allows some particles to pass through but not others.

Electrodialysis is one membrane process. It is based on the fact that dissolved salts are electrically charged. Some particles, such as sodium atoms, are positively charged. Others, such as chlorine atoms, are negatively charged. An electric current is passed through seawater. This causes positively charged atoms to move toward the negative pole of the electrical apparatus and negatively charged atoms to move toward the positive pole. The atoms then pass through semipermeable membranes, leaving behind pure water.

Another membrane process is reverse osmosis, which has become a popular technology for small- and medium-sized plants. Normally, if fresh water and salt water are on opposite sides of a semipermeable membrane, the fresh water passes, or diffuses, through the membrane. If pressure is applied to the salt water, however, the process is reversed: Water molecules diffuse out of the salt water into the fresh water.

SALTY ICE CUBES?

Sailors in wintery polar oceans need not worry if their ship's supply of drinking water runs low. It's probable that they are surrounded by fresh water. When ocean water freezes, the ice that forms does not contain any salt. The salt remains behind in unfrozen water. The ice can be removed from the ocean and rinsed off. When it melts, it will be very drinkable.

8

WATER POLLUTION

In mid-1991, a train derailed near Dunsmuir, California, alongside the Sacramento River. A tank car split open, spilling about 19,500 gallons (73,813 liters) of the pesticide metam sodium into the river. The chemical formed a stinking, bubbling green glob that moved 45 miles (72 kilometers) down the river, killing everything in its path. Hundreds of thousands of fish were killed, including at least 100,000 rainbow trout. Dragonflies, mayflies and other types of insects were killed. Plants in the river and along its edge were killed. Even creatures living beneath rocks on the river's bottom were killed. Then the green glob entered Shasta Lake, California's largest reservoir. No one knew what would happen next. Would the glob disperse and become harmless? Or would it poison the drinking water that flows from the lake into the state's water supply?

Metam sodium has been a popular pesticide for more than 30 years. It is used on farm soil before planting to kill weeds and insects. Despite metam sodium's known toxicity, the U.S. Department of Transportation did not classify it as a hazardous material. Therefore, the pesticide did not have to be transported in a specially protected tank car. The tank car that carried the metam sodium through California was of a type that the National Transportation Safety Board said had "a high incidence of failure" in accidents. Furthermore, the

Opposite page:
Pollution occurs in all kinds of water around the world. Although some serious pollutants can come from natural sources, most water pollution is the direct result of human activities such as industry, waste dumping and accidents.

RADON IN DRINKING WATER

Radon is an odorless, colorless gas that forms during the natural breakdown, or decay, of uranium. Because it is a gas, it can move through pores and cracks in the ground. It is also soluble in water and will dissolve into groundwater. When radon reaches the ground's surface, it disperses into the atmosphere. But if radon enters air or water inside a house, residents may be harmed.

Radon is radioactive. If enough radon is inhaled, it can damage lung tissue and cause cancer. In the United States, radon is believed to be a factor in an estimated 5,000 to 20,000 lung cancer deaths each year. Most of the risk occurs when radon seeps into homes from underlying soil—through cracks and other openings in the foundation. But some lung cancer deaths are thought to be caused by inhaling radon emitted by well water as it flows out of faucets and showerheads. In addition, other types of cancer may be caused by drinking radon-contaminated well water.

Homes can be tested for radon. If radon is detected in the air of a home, it is advisable to test the water supply if the home uses well water. If there is a significant amount of radon in the water, it should be removed before the water reaches the faucet. This is done by filtering the water through a device that contains granular activated carbon. Up to 99% of the radon attaches to the carbon particles.

tank car was not labeled. The train's crew did not know they were hauling a dangerous compound.

This type of incident makes the headlines and dramatizes the effects of pollution. People do not quickly forget television films of gasping, flapping, dying fish. They do not quickly forget newspaper photos of massive fish kills. But most water pollution is not visible.

Pollution Is Widespread

All water is subject to pollution. Pollution does not occur only in surface water; much of the world's groundwater also is polluted. In 1990, the U.S. Environmental Protection Agency (EPA) estimated that 10% of the nation's community drinking water wells had detectable residues of at least one pesticide, and more than 50% of the nation's wells contained nitrates.

Just because water contains contaminants does not prove that the water is harmful to human health. For example, the EPA said that less than 1% of the U.S. wells had unsafe levels of pesticide residues. On the other hand, much is not known about the long-term health risks of many chemicals. Frequently in the past, substances that were believed to be harmless turned out to be dangerous.

Some serious pollutants come from natural sources. For example, when groundwater filters through rocks rich in uranium deposits, it picks up uranium and radon, both of which can cause cancer.

Most water pollution, however, is caused by humans. The degree and kind of pollution caused by human activities vary greatly from place to place. Agricultural areas are more likely to experience contamination with fertilizers and pesticides than are urban areas. Countries that lack sewer systems and other sanitary facilities frequently find drinking water supplies contaminated with large amounts of fecal wastes.

Major Pollutants and Their Effects

Four main kinds of pollutants enter water supplies as a result of human activities: microorganisms, nutrients, toxic chemicals and heat.

Microorganisms

Food scraps and the excrement of humans and animals contain bacteria and other microorganisms. For example, it is estimated that the feces excreted in one day by one person contain one million coliform bacteria. These particular bacteria are not necessarily harmful. But the presence of coliform bacteria indicates that harmful species, including hard-to-detect viruses, may also be present.

Waterborne diseases claim most of their victims in areas that lack sanitation facilities. According to the U.N. Environment Programme, waterborne diseases cause an average of about 25,000 deaths a day in developing countries. Children are especially hard hit. A leading cause of illnesses among children in developing countries is diarrhea, an illness that is easily preventable or treatable in places with safe drinking water and good sanitation.

Cholera and typhoid fever, both caused by bacteria, and hepatitis A, caused by a virus, are generally spread through water and food contaminated with the feces or urine of people who have the diseases. Guinea worm disease infects up to 10 million people annually, mainly in India, Pakistan and 17 African countries. People drink water containing larval guinea worms. The worms grow within a victim's body until they measure 2 to 3 feet (.6 to .9 of a meter) long. About a year after the person drinks contaminated water, mature female worms produce ulcers, or openings, in the skin. This causes much pain and may cripple the person for months. If the person enters water, thousands of young larvae are released by the female worms, completing the cycle.

Nutrients

Sewage, agricultural runoff and some other wastes are rich in nitrogen and phosphorus. These chemicals are used by plants for growth. When the concentration of nitrogen and phosphorus compounds increases in a lake or other waterway, algae and aquatic plants grow much faster than normal. This rapid growth consumes more and more of the oxygen in the water. As oxygen levels fall, fish begin to sicken and die. If oxygen levels drop too low, almost all the fish and plant life in the water will disappear.

A KILLER DISEASE

For many centuries, cholera was a disease known only to Asia, where periodic outbreaks caused many thousands of deaths. Then, in the 19th century, travelers and soldiers carried the disease westward, through the Middle East and Russia into western Europe. From there it passed on to North America. Its reputation as a killer preceded it—with good reason. More than 100,000 Russians are believed to have died from cholera in 1830. Hardest hit were people in rapidly growing cities. In 1831, an epidemic raged through London, killing more than 50,000 people. The next year, a major outbreak struck New York, causing thousands of people to flee the city in steam-boats and stage-coaches.

No one knew what caused cholera or how it was spread. Some people believed it was caused by vapors given off by dead bodies. Others said that only people who broke the Sabbath and led immoral lives were susceptible to the disease. In some parts of France, poor people—who have always been more susceptible to cholera than rich people—believed that the government was deliberately poisoning them.

In the mid-1800s, people realized that cholera is spread primarily by drinking water and food supplies contaminated with human wastes. They found that contracting the disease could be largely prevented by purifying drinking water. But it wasn't until 1883 that the famous German bacteriologist, Robert Koch identified the cause of the disease: a bacterium that was named *Vibrio cholerae*. The bacteria are excreted in the fecal wastes of infected people.

As water and sewage systems were improved, the possibility of contaminating drinking water with sewage wastes declined. Cholera largely disappeared from developed countries. In poorer areas, however, periodic outbreaks have continued.

In 1991, a cholera epidemic struck in Peru. It was the first major outbreak of cholera in the Western Hemisphere in the 20th century. Within four months, more than 175,000 Peruvians had become ill and 1,300 had died. Meanwhile, the cholera had spread into Ecuador, Colombia, Brazil and Chile.

Many Peruvians take their drinking water from nearby rivers, which are also used to carry untreated human wastes to the sea. The vegetables they eat are grown on fields irrigated with untreated water from these same rivers. A raw fish dish called ceviche is a favorite among Peruvians, and many of the fish they eat are caught from waters contaminated by the wastes.

The United Nations estimates that 60% of Peru's 22 million people live in extreme poverty. A UNESCO (United Nations Educational, Scientific and Cultural Organization) repre-sentative said that 50% of the people do not have access to safe drinking water and 65% do not have piped sewage systems. The poor can safeguard against in-fection by washing their hands and food, by boiling drinking water and foods, and by buying safe water. But many poor people cannot afford to buy soap and heating fuel. Edgard Necochea, a health official for the Agency for International Development, commented, "When you have to buy water to drink, it is very difficult to think of using water to wash your hands."

The Pan American Health Organization calculated that it would cost $320 million a year for 10 years to build adequate water and sewage systems for Peru's 22 million inhabitants. For many countries, this is an insignificant amount of money. But Peru does not have such money. Thus, cholera is likely to continue to be a serious problem there.

The most common sign of excessive nutrients in water is an algal bloom—a massive concentration of algae. Algal blooms can harm all aquatic organisms, including commer-cially valuable fish. In 1988, a foul-smelling algal bloom began killing fish off the coast of Sweden. Water currents carried the bloom northward. Soon the bloom threatened fish farms along the Norwegian coast. Large numbers of cages containing young salmon had to be towed deep into Norwegian fjords to save the fish. Marine biologists were quite certain that this algae bloom was caused by excessive amounts of nutrients dumped into the ocean by human activities.

Hazardous Chemicals

Many chemicals used by humans are dangerous because of their effects on living things. Among the most dangerous of these chemicals are heavy metals, petroleum and certain pesticides.

Heavy metals are metallic elements such as mercury, lead, arsenic, chromium, zinc, copper and cadmium. Many heavy metals cause cancer. Heavy metals can also cause other health problems. Lead causes birth defects and learning disabilities. Mercury damages nerves and can cause skin rashes. Cadmium damages the liver and kidneys.

Oil pollution harms every type of aquatic organism, from bacteria and algae to fish and mammals. Some organisms are killed almost immediately. Others die slowly or suffer from long-term problems, such as respiratory ailments and reproductive defects. Oil can interfere with processes at wastewater treatment plants by killing bacteria used to treat the sewage. Oil that seeps into groundwater can contaminate drinking supplies with toxic compounds.

As discussed in Chapter 5, many pesticides are toxic to people and wildlife. Some accumulate in the bodies of living organisms until concentrations are high enough to interfere with reproduction and cause other physical damage.

Heat

Power stations and factories draw great quantities of cold water from waterways for cooling purposes. Heat is transferred from hot equipment to the water. If the heated water is returned directly to rivers or lakes it can interfere with the water's ecology. As the temperature of the water increases, its ability to hold oxygen decreases. Organisms that require high concentrations of oxygen, such as trout, can no longer survive in the habitat. Heat also can kill fish or prevent them from reproducing. This is called thermal pollution.

Sources of Human Pollution

Until fairly recently, water pollution was thought to be caused mainly by cities and factories. When people wanted to illustrate water pollution, they pointed to pipes that emptied a city's raw sewage or a factory's oily wastes. But pipes that discharge industrial wastes are not the main source of water pollution.

Pollution that comes from a specific source, such as a sewer or factory pipe, is called point pollution. Pollution that comes from diffuse sources is called nonpoint pollution. Runoff from farm fields, roadways, construction sites, deforested lands and mining operations are examples of nonpoint pollution. The sources of nonpoint pollutants are often difficult to locate and control.

Communities

Every time a person flushes a toilet, takes a shower or washes clothes, sewage is created. Sewage is the watery waste flushed from toilets, bathtubs, washing machines, sinks and dishwashers. The amount of sewage created each year is staggering. An estimated 14.4 billion gallons (54.5 billion liters) of

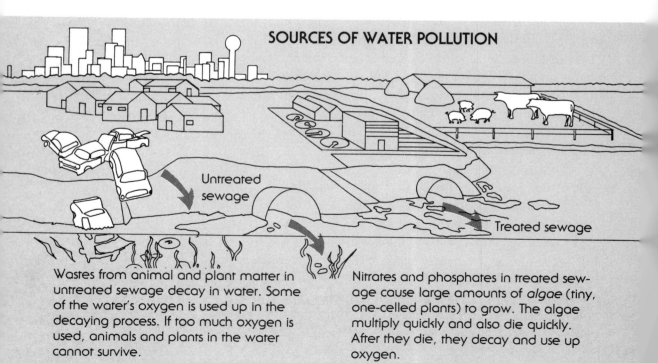

SOURCES OF WATER POLLUTION

Untreated sewage

Treated sewage

Wastes from animal and plant matter in untreated sewage decay in water. Some of the water's oxygen is used up in the decaying process. If too much oxygen is used, animals and plants in the water cannot survive.

Nitrates and phosphates in treated sewage cause large amounts of *algae* (tiny, one-celled plants) to grow. The algae multiply quickly and also die quickly. After they die, they decay and use up oxygen.

sewage are created just by U.S. homes *every day!* Sewage usually contains high levels of bacteria, viruses and compounds containing nitrogen and phosphorus. It may also contain toxic chemicals, such as those found in paint thinners, wood preservatives, and certain household cleaners.

In developed nations, much of the sewage flows through pipes to wastewater treatment plants, where many of the contaminants are removed or rendered harmless. In developing countries, about 75% of the population lack adequate sanitary facilities. Most sewage is dumped into streams and rivers. In India, for example, 114 towns and cities dump untreated sewage into the Ganges, one of the country's holiest rivers.

Communities also are the source of nonpoint pollution. Rainwater and melting snow that run off lawns and golf courses carry fertilizers and pesticides. Runoff from streets carries oil, heavy metals and chemicals used to melt ice.

Many communities dispose of solid wastes in open dumps or huge landfills. As water seeps through the wastes, it picks up dissolved or suspended contaminants. If this leachate is not stopped, it can enter water supplies.

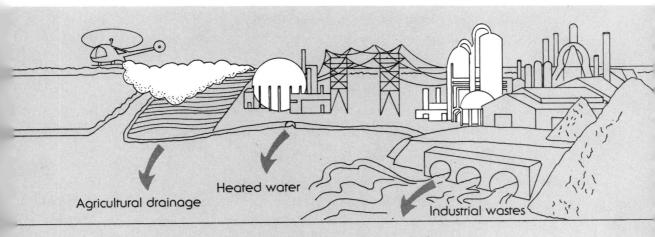

Agricultural drainage   Heated water   Industrial wastes

Agricultural drainage includes animal wastes, which decay; fertilizers, which increase the growth of algae; and pesticides, which kill animals and plants.

Most heated water comes from industries that use water for cooling. Animals and plants that are used to living in cooler water are killed.

Many industries produce chemicals, wastes from animal and plant matter, and hundreds of other subtances. They ruin water by upsetting natural cycles.

MINIMATA DISEASE

Methyl mercury once was used widely by North American pulp mills to kill bacteria and fungi that grew on machinery. The compound was applied to the machinery, then rinsed off with water and dumped into streams and rivers. Early in 1970, fish taken from Lake Erie, which borders both Canada and the United States, were found to contain large quantities of methyl mercury. Dangerous levels of the compound were also found in fish from lakes Ontario and Champlain, as well as the St. Lawrence and Niagara rivers. Eating fish from these waters had to be banned, to protect people from Minimata disease.

Mercury poisoning is sometimes called Minimata disease because of a tragic episode that occurred during the 1950s in Minimata, a coastal fishing community in Japan. Some 700 people in Minimata died excruciating deaths; 9,000 others suffered permanent brain damage. The cause was determined to be a mercury compound that had been dumped into the sea by a nearby plastics factory. The mercury, in the form of methyl mercury, accumulated in fish and shellfish. Eventually, the contaminated seafood was caught and eaten by the people of Minimata.

People who change their own car and truck oil often dispose of the used oil by dumping it on the ground or down a sewer drain. This oil is actually more harmful than crude oil because it contains hazardous additives. It is estimated that Americans incorrectly dump some 260 million gallons (984 million liters) of used oil each year—more than 20 times as much as entered Alaskan waters in 1989 when the *Exxon Valdez* struck a reef in Prince William Sound.

Agriculture and Aquaculture

Agriculture is the most common source of nonpoint pollution in many countries. The overapplication of irrigation water creates runoff that washes into waterways, carrying fertilizers, salts and other chemicals. As water seeps into the soil, it may carry chemical pollutants to groundwater supplies. The United States, Denmark and France are among the many countries that have reported widespread nitrate contamination of groundwater.

Seepage from the manure of animals raised in feedlots and barnyards also pollutes water supplies. Wastes from fish farms can pollute surrounding waters and cause disease outbreaks.

Industry

Industry uses much less water than agriculture but it pollutes it more. According to the U.S. Environmental Protection Agency, manufacturers in the United States released 9.7 billion pounds (4.4 billion kilograms) of toxic chemicals into rivers and other surface waters during 1987. Large as this amount was, it covered only 300 chemicals; hundreds of additional toxic chemicals did not have to be reported. Also, only manufacturers that used more than 10,000 pounds (4,536 kilograms) or produced more than 75,000 pounds (34,000 kilograms) of the chemicals were required to report to the EPA. And about 25% of the companies that were required to report did not do so.

Many industries dispose of wastes, including hazardous chemicals, in landfills that are subject to leaching. Groundwater is also contaminated by chemicals that seep from underground storage tanks, pipelines and injection wells.

Surface and underground mining operations produce heavy metals and other pollutants. For instance, the discharge of mercury from gold-mining operations has contaminated streams in Brazil. Seepage from abandoned and inactive mines polluted thousands of miles of streams in the United States. Uranium mines, weapons factories and nuclear power plants are sources of radioactive materials.

The transportation and electric power industries are other major sources of pollutants. Ships annually spill millions of gallons of oil into waterways, either accidentally or when flushing their holds. Ships discharge sewage and garbage into rivers and oceans. Vehicles and electric generating plants that burn fossil fuels are the primary sources of the pollutants that form acid rain. Some acid rain falls directly into lakes and rivers. Acid rain that falls on land leaches toxic metals from the soil into ground- and surface waters.

Fossil-fuel and nuclear electric generating plants are the main sources of thermal pollution. Metal manufacturers, chemical plants and petrochemical producers also discharge large quantities of heated water.

Economic Costs of Pollution

Water pollution has killed, and caused illness in, untold millions of people who could otherwise have led productive lives. It has destroyed natural habitats and the plants and animals that depend on those habitats for their survival. Fishermen have become unemployed because fishing grounds have been destroyed by pollution. Pollution has made lakes, rivers and beaches unsuitable for swimming and other recreational purposes. This has harmed resort hotels, and other businesses that rely on recreational users of waterways.

Treating water to remove impurities is expensive. It costs millions of dollars to build and operate a water or wastewater treatment facility. The greater the amount of pollution, the more expensive the treatment. And even small amounts of pollution can require treatment of large amounts of water. For example, just one gallon (3.78 liters) of used oil can contaminate one million gallons (3.78 million liters) of drinking water.

9

MAKING WATER SAFE TO USE

In a modern city in a wealthy country, a child turns a faucet to obtain drinking water that is free from contaminants and safe to drink. In a poor rural area in a developing country, a child may have to walk miles to get drinking water from a well, and this water may be dangerously polluted. The child in the modern city has access to toilets connected to sewer systems that carry wastes to treatment plants. The poor rural child may not have access to toilets of any kind and may have to use roadways, fields and streams as sewers. It is the dream and the goal of many governments, international agencies and private organizations to provide the poor rural child with the same access to safe water and sanitation facilities as that enjoyed by the child in the modern city.

Modern Water Supply Systems

A water supply system collects, treats, stores and distributes drinkable water. Water is drawn from a stream or pumped from wells that tap underground aquifers. Surface water flows through intake works where a series of screens removes debris. First, coarse screens intercept branches, ice and other large objects. Further along the conduit are finely meshed screens designed to remove small suspended material.

Opposite page: Water in public water supplies must undergo a series of treatments and purifications before it is ready for human consumption. Debris, small suspended material, bacteria, algae and other chemical compounds must all be removed before water is ingested or used for irrigation. Here, water is treated in a series of vats at a plant in Oakland, California.

Microscopic algae are common in surface waters. If the algae are not removed, the water has an objectionable taste. Small quantities of the chemical copper sulfate are added to the water to kill the algae. Bacteria may be removed by letting the water sink through a sand filter. The most widely used method of disinfection, however, is the addition of chlorine, which may be done at several steps in the treatment process. Chlorine kills harmful bacteria and also destroys algae and undesirable organic compounds.

Another treatment is aeration: mixing the water with air so that oxygen in the air can combine with compounds that may give the water an offensive taste or smell. Aeration may be accomplished by injecting air into the water, mechanically mixing the water, spraying the water into the air or letting it flow down artificial waterfalls.

Filters of activated carbon are used to remove organic chemicals. The chemicals cling to the surface of the carbon granules. Periodically, the carbon filters are replaced with fresh filters.

Groundwater supplies are often "hard." That is, the water contains dissolved minerals collected while it flowed through the ground. Certain calcium and magnesium compounds create the biggest problems; if not removed, they prevent soap from lathering. Generally, hard water is "softened" by adding lime and soda ash, which react with the calcium and magnesium compounds to form substances that settle out or can be removed by filters.

When treatment is complete, the water is distributed through a system of pipes to users. In some places, the water flows downhill, through the force of gravity. Usually, however, pumps are needed to push the water through the distribution system.

Among the most difficult problems facing water suppliers is removing or breaking down modern chemical pollutants. Substantial, expensive treatment may be needed. In the United States as of 1991, there were federal standards for 60 drinking water contaminants. These standards set maximum contaminant levels for various pesticides, PCBs, toxic metals, toluene and other volatile organic compounds, nitrates and nitrites, asbestos and for other substances. Some 80,000 drinking water systems in the nation—all those supplying drinking water to at least 25 people—are required to meet these standards. They must monitor for the contaminants, sometimes as often as every three months, to ensure that the standards are met on a continuing basis.

Wastewater Collection and Disposal

After people use water in their homes, schools, hospitals, office buildings and factories, the water becomes wastewater. It can be collected and treated to remove pollutants.

Septic Systems

Septic systems are commonly used by houses in suburban or rural areas. These systems depend on natural processes to treat sewage. Wastewater flows through a pipe from the house to a watertight tank buried in the ground. Solid matter settles to the bottom of the tank, where bacteria digest organic materials. The semi-liquid residue that remains is called sludge; it must periodically be pumped out of the tank. The sludge can be treated and used as a soil conditioner or it may be dumped in a landfill or incinerated.

The liquid part of the sewage slowly flows out of the upper portion of the septic tank through perforated pipes and into the surrounding soil. Bacteria in the soil decompose some of the wastes. Other undissolved solids cling to soil particles; some contain nutrients that can be absorbed and used by plants.

Not all the substances in sewage are rendered harmless in a septic system. Septic systems are a major source of groundwater contamination, especially when they are poorly constructed or poorly placed, or when they do not function properly.

Wastewater Treatment Plants

In cities and towns, wastewater from homes, businesses, and many factories is discharged into pipes that lead to a waste-

WHO HAS SAFE WATER AND SANITATION?

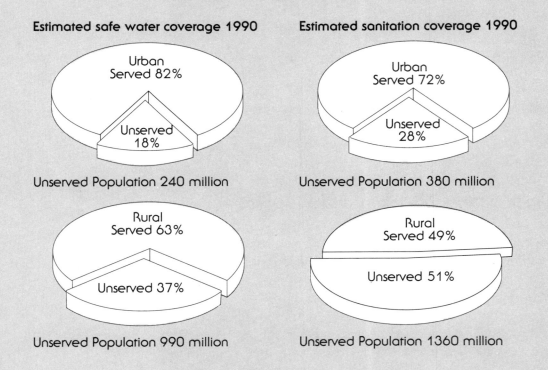

Estimated safe water coverage 1990

Urban
Served 82%

Unserved
18%

Unserved Population 240 million

Rural
Served 63%

Unserved 37%

Unserved Population 990 million

Estimated sanitation coverage 1990

Urban
Served 72%

Unserved
28%

Unserved Population 380 million

Rural
Served 49%

Unserved 51%

Unserved Population 1360 million

The target of universal access to safe water and sanitation for the year 2000 will be one of the most difficult to achieve. The rate of expansion of water supply achieved during the 1980s will have to be increased by a factor of two and a half during the 1990s if the goal is to be reached.

Source: UNIFEC estimates based on WHO data.

water treatment plant. Here, the wastewater is treated to make it fit for discharge into the environment. Wastewater treatment facilities vary widely in efficiency and in the types of treatment performed. Three kinds of treatment are possible: primary, secondary and tertiary.

Primary treatment is largely a mechanical process that removes about 30% of the pollutants in the water. As the sewage enters the treatment plant, it flows through a series of screens to remove branches, rags and other floating objects. Some plants grind these objects so they remain in the sewage, to be removed later in a settling tank. Next, the sewage enters a grit chamber, where solids such as gravel and sand sink to the bottom. Then the sewage enters settling tanks, where suspended matter settles out of the flow, forming sludge. In some plants, the remaining liquid is treated with chlorine to destroy disease-causing bacteria and then discharged.

Secondary treatment consists mostly of biological processes. After receiving primary treatment, the sewage enters an aeration tank where it is mixed with bacteria-rich sludge. The bacteria digest organic matter in the sewage. The sewage then flows into a secondary sedimentation tank, where the sludge settles out. The remaining effluent can then be treated with chlorine and discharged. At this point, about 85% of the pollutants have been removed.

Increasingly, wastewater treatment facilities perform not only primary and secondary treatment but also tertiary treatment. Tertiary treatment consists mostly of chemical processes. Electrodialysis, distillation, reverse osmosis and other processes are used to remove nitrates, phosphorus, ozone, organic chemicals, heavy metals and other dissolved substances. Following such treatment, about 95% of the pollutants in the original sewage have been removed.

Large amounts of sludge are produced during treatment. Some communities dump untreated sludge into oceans, where it can cause much damage to fish and other organisms. Other communities bury it in the ground. With treatment, however, sludge can be used to condition soil. It often is used to reclaim stripmined lands and other barren areas.

Alternative Systems

Instead of using conventional wastewater treatment plants, some communities purify sewage with marshland plants, hungry snails and other organisms. The communities have built artificial wetlands in which natural biological processes remove impurities at comparatively low costs. At the same time, the wetlands provide habitats for a variety of birds, mammals and other wildlife.

In Arcata, California, sewage flows into the city's sewage plant, where it receives primary treatment. Then it is channeled into two large oxidation ponds where biological de-

BOTTLED WATER

Millions of people in the United States pay up to 1,200 times more for drinking water than is necessary. Instead of drinking tap water, they drink bottled water. In 1989, Americans consumed 1.7 billion gallons (6.4 billion liters) of bottled water.

One reason for buying bottled water is the belief that it is safer than tap water. But researchers at the University of Iowa analyzed 39 samples of bottled water and concluded that the quality of typical bottled waters sold in Iowa was about the same as the quality of the state's public water supplies.

A report from the U.S. General Accounting Office indicated that some bottled waters may actually be less safe than tap water. Some contain higher levels of potentially harmful contaminants than are allowed for public drinking water. One government survey found that 31% of the bottled water tested exceeded standards for bacterial content.

composition takes place. Next, the effluent is chlorinated. It flows into marshes filled with cattails, bullrushes and other plants that have the ability to remove toxic chemicals and metals from the water. Bacteria and other microorganisms living on the plant roots feed on organic matter in the effluent. About two months after the water leaves the treatment plant, it flows into Humboldt Bay. It is cleaner than the water already in the bay!

Providence, Rhode Island, is treating some wastes in a special greenhouse. Sewage flows through a series of fiberglass vats filled with bacteria, snails, fish and marshland plants such as water hyacinths, Egyptian papyrus and watercress. The effluent becomes progressively cleaner and clearer. Within several days it can be discharged. As with the effluent from Arcata Marsh, it is as clean as—or cleaner than—effluent from conventional treatment plants.

An International Decade

Few developing countries can afford the high-tech water-supply and sanitation systems typically found in Europe, North America, Japan and other developed lands. Millions of people must spend hours of every day walking miles to fill buckets with water—water that is often polluted. Most wastes, including human excrement, are dumped into rivers and streams. Cities that have piped water supplies often lose up to half the water through leaks in pipes and taps.

The International Drinking Water Supply and Sanitation Decade was launched in 1981 by the United Nations. Its goal was to provide safe water and sanitation for all humans by 1990. During the following 10 years, thousands of low-cost, sustainable structures were installed. Wells were dug and fitted with handpumps. Latrines and sewer drains were constructed.

When technologies used in wealthier lands proved to be unsuitable or too expensive for developing countries, people came up with alternatives. In Thailand, bamboo was substituted for expensive steel to reinforce the walls of rainwater storage tanks. In Burkina Faso, a simple wheelbarrow-like device was designed for carrying water. In India, communities adopted the pour-flush latrine, a low-cost structure consisting of a squatting pan connected to two leach pits. Excrement flows into one of the pits. When that pit fills after several years, it is closed and the second pit is opened for use. Within two years, the wastes in the first pit turn into a solid residue that can be used as fertilizer.

In earlier attempts to provide communities with new water and sanitation systems, it became obvious that installing equipment was not enough. Many development efforts failed because of lack of routine maintenance and a scarcity of spare parts. Decade officials realized that beneficiaries had to view the systems as belonging to their community. The people had to be involved in planning and installing the systems, and they had to accept responsibility for managing the systems. During the decade, community members were taught how to maintain and repair the facilities. They were given lessons in health and hygiene and were encouraged to share these lessons with their children.

The Decade achieved much success. During the 1980s, more than 1.3 billion people in developing countries gained access to safe drinking water. Nearly 750 million got improved sanitation services. Well before the 1980s ended, however, it became obvious that there was no chance that the Decade's original goal would be achieved. While water-supply and sanitation facilities were growing in number, so was human population. By 1990, the percentage of people in Africa with access to safe, adequate water supplies was 64.5%. The percentage of people having access to appropriate sanitary facilities was 52.5%. But because of population growth, the total number of people without access to these services actually rose: 20 million more people in Africa lacked safe water and 30 million more lacked adequate sanitation than 10 years earlier.

In 1990, 1.2 billion people in developing countries still needed basic water services; 1.7 billion people lacked decent sanitation. U.N. agencies and other international organizations have renewed efforts to implement needed programs under a campaign called Safe Water 2000.

10

CONSERVING WATER

In 1990, the U.S. Environmental Protection Agency (EPA) vetoed a proposed dam on the South Platte River near Denver, Colorado. The project, which would have been the most expensive dam in U.S. history, was designed to increase water supplies for Denver and nearby communities. It would have created the largest lake in Colorado, flooding 24 miles (39 kilometers) of freely flowing river, valuable wetlands and an area of great natural beauty and abundant wildlife. LaJuana S. Wilcher, EPA assistant administrator for water, said that "less environmentally damaging, practicable alternatives exist." Among those alternatives: stronger efforts to implement water conservation measures, so that the demand for new water supplies is reduced.

Every water user—including farms, industries and individuals—can cut back on water use. Some efforts are simple and take no effort. Others are more complex and may be costly. Often, however, water conservation actually saves money.

Conservation on the Farm

Improved farming techniques and irrigation practices allow farmers to make more efficient use of water supplies. Contour

Opposite page: Water conservation is essential to the survival of our planet. Improved farming techniques, conservation by industry and individuals and treatment of wastewater will help ensure a plentiful water supply for future generations.

AN UNDERPRICED RESOURCE

In many countries, governments subsidize the cost of delivering water to farmers. In Pakistan, for example, farmers pay only about 13% of the actual cost of the water they use.

In the United States, the government supplies water to more than 10 million acres (4 million hectares) of irrigated land in the western states; 85% or more of the cost of this water is paid by taxpayers. Because the farmers pay so little of the true cost, they do not have an incentive to adopt efficient irrigation methods and other conservation practices. Many waste precious resources. They use flood irrigation, covering their land completely with up to six times as much water as is needed. In addition to wasting water, this creates runoff that carries fertilizers and other pollutants into nearby rivers, harming wildlife and increasing water treatment costs for communities downstream.

Sandra Postel of the World-watch Institute explains, "Since agriculture uses such an enormous quantity of water, conserving even a small portion of it can meet a large share of new urban needs. Raising water prices to reflect the true cost of deliveries is a critical step toward this end."

plowing and terracing limit runoff and increase the amount of water available to plant roots.

Farmers should grow crops that are appropriate for the climate in their region. Some crops are much "thirstier" than others; they require a lot of water. Rice, alfalfa and cotton are examples. Together with irrigated pasture for livestock, these crops are the biggest water users in California—a state plagued by water shortages caused by growing populations, an arid climate and an extended drought. California's alfalfa crop, which is raised for cattle feed, uses almost 4.1 million acre-feet of water a year. One acre-foot equals 325,848 gallons (1,233,432 liters)—the annual consumption of two typical California households.

Even growing different varieties of the same crop may cut water needs. For example, a new variety of cotton needs 20% less water than commonly grown varieties.

More Efficient Irrigation

Since irrigation accounts for the bulk of most countries' water use, switching to more efficient irrigation techniques can save enormous amounts of water. A technique called low-energy precision application (LEPA) uses a nozzle that delivers water closer to the ground and in larger drops than

FOOD AND WATER
The Solutions

Water is the Earth's most vital resource.

Right: Fertile hillsides benefit from terracing in Indonesia.
Above: Amaranth plants blossom in Colorado.

FARMERS ARE TURNING to a variety of practices in an effort to ensure food for future generations. Contour plowing, terracing and other conservation practices slow erosion. Biological pesticides, such as tiny worms used to control Japanese beetles, are replacing chemical pesticides. Previously underused crops, such as amaranth and quinoa, are being grown more widely. Hope also comes from laboratories, where scientists are creating new types of crops—crops that are more productive, disease-resistant and able to grow well in arid conditions.

WORLDWIDE EFFORTS ARE UNDERWAY TO CONSERVE the genetic diversity of plants and animals raised for food. Seed banks have been established to save seeds of wild and rarely used varieties because these varieties contain potentially valuable genes not found in more widely raised varieties. Rare breeds of cattle, sheep, pigs and other domesticated animals are also being saved, as are stocks of wild fish. Other efforts to ensure food for the future include growing crops on previously underutilized land, expanding aquaculture, introducing higher-yield forage crops and developing ways to fight plant and animal diseases without harming the environment or the people who eventually eat those plants and animals.

Far left: A New York City resident turns an urban space into a bountiful garden. *Above:* A farmer vaccinates cattle with an injection gun.

Vast amounts of water are used for agriculture, industrial processes and such personal activities as taking baths and washing clothes. During use, the water becomes polluted with various wastes. If dumped into the environment, the polluted water can cause great harm. But if the wastes are removed, the water can be reused. Wastewater treatment plants use various mechanical, biological and chemical processes to remove impurities from water. The greater the amount of treatment, the purer the water. Indeed, with sufficient treatment, sewage can be turned into drinking water. The wastes, or sludge, removed from the sewage can be used as a soil conditioner on farms, gardens and in barren areas such as stripmined land. As populations and water use increase, the need for efficient wastewater treatment becomes more and more critical.

A wastewater holding pond glistens in the evening sun at a Delaware treatment facility.

A young boy drinks from a fountain at Golden Gate Park in San Francisco, California.

ALL WATER USERS CAN CONSERVE WATER and thus help ensure sufficient supplies for the future. Farmers can switch to more efficient methods of irrigation. Cattle ranchers can hold and treat animal wastes rather than allowing the wastes to seep into rivers and aquifers. Factories can reuse water several times before discharging it into the environment, thereby reducing the amount of wastewater that needs treatment. Individuals can install water-saving toilets and showerheads in their homes.

traditional sprinkler systems. This decreases the amount of water lost to evaporation. Some farmers in Texas cut the average amount of irrigation water they used by 28% between 1974 and 1987 because they adopted LEPA and other practices.

Drip systems consist of a network of perforated plastic pipes that are installed on or below the surface of the soil. Water is delivered in needed quantities directly to the crop's roots; very little of it evaporates and the problem of soil salinity is reduced. In addition, fertilizers can be dissolved in the irrigation water, decreasing the amount of chemicals spread on fields and helping to avoid the possibility of groundwater contamination. The systems allow farmers to control carefully the amount of water and nutrients given to crops, which often leads to improved crop yields. Farmers experimenting with drip systems in Israel's Negev Desert have increased crop yields up to 80% over those achieved with sprinkler systems.

In conventional furrow irrigation, water is siphoned from large ditches and run into the furrows between rows of crops. The farmer keeps the irrigation valve open until water reaches the lower end of the furrows. On large fields, this may take many hours. During that time, the upper end of the furrows receives more water than is needed by the crops. A more efficient system is surge irrigation. Instead of a constant flow, water is delivered in surges. The first surge soaks into the first section of the furrows. During the following moments when the soil is exposed to air, it partially seals itself. When a second surge travels over the furrows, it flows faster over the partially sealed soil surface and irrigates the next section. The process continues until the entire length of the furrows is irrigated. The process spreads water more uniformly along the furrows and is much faster than the conventional method.

Lining irrigation canals that carry water to fields can greatly reduce the amount of water lost to seepage. Automating irrigation systems reduces loss because computers can set optimal water flow, taking into account such factors as wind speed and the amount of moisture already in the soil. Computers also can detect leaks in the systems.

Conservation will not be sufficient to meet the water needs of the world's growing populations. Additional sources of water will also have to be developed. As a project in Oman demonstrates, even fog can be an important source of water.

In Oman's southwestern province of Dhofar, surface and groundwater are scarce. People living in hilly rural villages have no easy access to water. But for three months each year, the mountains are covered with fog. Research scientists placed metal storage tanks, each with a capacity of 713 gallons (2,700 liters) on the hills. A large vertical screen with plastic mesh was erected over each tank. The small fog droplets hit the screen and gradually join together to form larger drops, which run down the mesh into the tank. The amount of water collected depends on the thickness of the fog, how long it remains over the hills and the speed of the wind. Altitude is also a factor. During one experiment, researchers measured the amount of water collected by tanks at altitudes of 1,575 feet (480 meters) and 3,018 feet (920 meters). Both tanks were topped by screens with an area of 11 square feet (1 square meter). Over a period of several months, the screen at the lower elevation yielded 1.6 gallons (6 liters) of fog water a day. The screen at the higher elevation yielded 21 gallons (80 liters) a day.

The water can be used for agriculture, drinking and many other uses. Ecologist Robert Whitcombe, who is with Oman's Planning Committee for Development and Environment in the Southern Region, wants to reforest the hills and use some of the water to irrigate young trees. When the trees mature in several years, they too will become fog collectors. They will collect enough water to irrigate themselves and perhaps even to recharge underground aquifers. One hillside tree intercepted 15,850 gallons (60,000 liters) of water during the 1989 monsoon season!

Conservation by Industry

A large portion of the water used for industrial purposes can be reused several times before being discharged into the environment. This decreases the amount of water withdrawn from rivers and other sources. It also decreases the amount of wastewater that requires treatment. In making paper, for example, large amounts of water are mixed with pulp. When the mixture enters the papermaking machine it is actually 99% water and 1% fiber. Through a series of screening and rolling steps, the water is squeezed out. Traditionally, paper mills have discharged the water into nearby rivers. Now, some of the mills have equipment that collects the water and reuses it. In Sweden, the pulp and paper industry accounts for 80% of industrial water use. When Swedish mills introduced ways to reuse water, water use was cut in half—at the same time that production doubled.

In Kansas City, Missouri, an Armco steel mill uses water 16 times before discharging it. As a result, it uses only 12 cubic yards (9 cubic meters) of water for each ton of steel it produces. Many other steel mills use up to 260 cubic yards (200 cubic meters) of water per ton of steel produced.

In 1991, IBM opened a wastewater treatment plant at its facility in San Jose, California, to purify groundwater that had been contaminated by wastes from the company's underground storage tanks. The plant produces 770,000 gallons (2,915,000 liters) of water daily—about half the amount of water needed by the IBM facility.

New, water-efficient processes can replace water-guzzleup processes. Ultrasonics Products, a California company, has developed a dishwasher for restaurants that uses ultrasound, high-frequency sound waves and only a small amount of water to remove food particles.

Conservation at Home

In the United States, the typical person uses between 55 and 75 gallons (208 and 284 liters) of water each day. Most of this water is used in the bathroom: 40% is used to flush toilets,

Water-saving showerheads are inexpensive and easy to install. If every home in the United States installed a low-flow showerhead, it would save an estimated 250 million gallons (946 million liters) of water every day.

BE A WATER SAVER!

Water conservation is something that everyone can practice. Here are some tips on how you can reduce water consumption in your home:

• Wash only full loads in washing machines and dishwashers. Use only the cycles needed to do the job.
• Wash hand laundry in batches instead of one item at a time. Do not use running water.
• Do not let the water run continuously while brushing your teeth, or washing your face.

• Try to reduce the length of your showers.
• Install flow-reducing devices in showerheads and faucets.
• Install a toilet dam or other water-saving tank device.
• Do not use the toilet as a waste basket to dispose of cigarette butts, facial tissues, etc.
• Dispose of garbage in a garbage can; avoid using garbage disposal units attached to sinks.
• Thaw frozen foods ahead of time in the refrigerator rather than using running water to quick-thaw them.

• Let ice trays sit out a few minutes to loosen cubes, rather than putting them under running water.
• Keep a bottle of water in the refrigerator instead of letting the tap run to get a cool drink.
• Insulate hot water pipes to reduce the amount of water that must run to get hot water from a faucet.
• Fix leaks and drips from faucets, hoses, etc. Most repairs involve a simple replacement of washers or other parts available at home supply stores.

30% is used in bathroom sinks and showers, 15% is used to do laundry, 10% is used in the kitchen and 5% flows from outside spigots.

Studies indicate that residential water use in the United States could easily be cut by one-third. Perhaps the biggest water guzzler is the toilet. A standard American toilet uses 5 to 7 gallons (19 to 27 liters) every time it is flushed. In contrast, ultra low-flush toilets empty the bowl using only 0.5 to 1.5 gallons (2 to 6 liters) of water.

Another water saver is the low-flow aerator. When attached to a faucet or showerhead, it reduces water flow by 50%. However, because the device mixes air into the water, the flow actually feels stronger. If every U.S. home installed aerators, the nation would save an estimated 250 million gallons (946 million liters) or more of water every day!

Enormous amounts of water are lost from leakage through pipes and faucets. A pinhole leak in a water pipe may seem insignificant, but it can waste 170 gallons (644 liters) a day—enough to wash your face 170 times!

Home gardeners can conserve water by allowing grass to grow higher before mowing it and by planting drought-resistant varieties. Watering lawns and gardens early in the morning or at dusk minimizes water loss through evaporation. Placing mulch around the base of trees, shrubs and garden plants also reduces evaporation.

Recycling

Almost all the wastes produced by people contain materials that can be recycled or reused. Recycling offers many benefits, among them the chance to save water. Making beverage cans and other products from recycled aluminum instead of aluminum ore cuts water pollution by 97%. Substituting scrap steel for virgin materials cuts water pollution 76% and water use 40%. Making paper from recycled materials cuts water pollution 35% and water use 58%.

Recycling is a multi-step process. It begins with individuals and communities who save and collect recyclable materials. Industries have to adapt their procedures to use the scrap. Then, people have to buy and use products made from recycled materials—rather than products made from virgin materials.

Water Fights

In many parts of the world, particularly during periods of drought, water supplies are insufficient to meet everyone's demands. As a result, conflicts arise. In the United States, several states along the Missouri River went to court in 1990, after nearly three years of drought caused a marked decline in river flow. People in Kansas and other downstream states wanted water to be released from reservoirs upstream. They said the water was needed to maintain river levels, so that barges carrying grain, fertilizers and other freight could operate. But North and South Dakota objected, saying that the release of upstream water would interfere with the spawning of walleye, a popular game fish, and with the area's economically important recreation industry. Fortunately, nature intervened: Heavy rains fell downstream, resolving the problem at least temporarily.

Less likely to be resolved is the conflict between Southern California and its neighbors. Los Angeles and surrounding communities long ago overtapped their groundwater and river resources. The area depends on water piped in from distant places: the Colorado River, more than 200 miles (322 kilometers) away; Mono Lake, 300 miles (483 kilometers) away; and the Feather River, nearly 600 miles (966 kilometers) away. All three sources will supply less water during the coming years than expected—at the same time that Southern California's population is exploding. For example, for decades Arizona fought in court for a larger share of the water from the Colorado. It finally won its case. When the Central Arizona Project is completed, Arizona will take millions of gallons of water that Southern California wants.

Water conflicts frequently cross national boundaries. About 40% of the world's population depends on water from a neighboring country. If an upstream country increases the amount of water it withdraws from a river, people in downstream countries receive less water to meet their needs. If an upstream country dumps sewage and chemical wastes into the river, people in downstream countries who depend on the river for drinking supplies suffer.

Turkey is building the Ataturk Dam on the Euphrates River, which runs from Turkey into Syria and Iraq before joining the Tigris River. The dam is a key factor in a large development program for southeastern Turkey. By the year 2005, the dam is supposed to irrigate about 6,600 square miles (17,160 square kilometers) of land and generate 27 billion kilowatt/hours of electricity each year. But Iraq and Syria are concerned about the effects that the dam will have on their use of water from the Euphrates.

Egypt's entire population—some 55 million people—depends on the Nile River for its water and electricity. Most of the river's flow comes from the Blue Nile, a tributary that rises in the highlands of western Ethiopia. If Ethiopia builds dams on the Blue Nile, might this decrease the amount of water available to Egypt?

As populations increase and the world grows thirstier, competition for water is expected to increase. Wise management of water resources, including water and soil conservation, will be essential if explosive conflicts are to be avoided.

Coordinated water resource policies are needed. An important step in this direction is the Zambezi Action Plan, signed in 1987. It calls for a unified approach to water management among the eight African nations that share the waters of the Zambezi River and its tributaries. These rivers drain about 540,000 square miles (1.4 million square kilometers) of almost the entire central southern region of the continent. Among the plan's priorities are the provision of drinking water and sanitation, soil and forest conservation, watershed management, energy projects, wildlife conservation and fisheries projects.

Commitments for the Future

Important steps have been taken toward assuring future generations of sufficient supplies of food and water. But much more must be done. Nations, communities, scientists and ordinary people must work together if land degradation, water and air pollution, empty aquifers, loss of biodiversity and other threats are to be successfully combatted.

"Never has humanity faced so crucial a decade as the 1990s," said Mostafa Kamel Tolba, executive director of the United Nations Environmental Programme. "The decisions—and, even more important, the actions—taken over these ten short years will determine the shape of the world for centuries. The very fate of life hangs upon them."

GLOSSARY

acre-foot The amount of water needed to flood one acre with water to a depth of one foot. It equals 325,848 gallons (1,233,432 liters).

agronomist A scientist who specializes in field crops.

aquaculture The raising of fish and other water organisms for consumption, as contrasted to harvesting these organisms from the wild.

aquifer An underground region saturated with water.

biological control The use of insects and other organisms to kill or otherwise control pest populations.

biological magnification The concentration of certain substances up a food chain. This is an important mechanism in concentrating pesticides and heavy metals in organisms such as birds and fish.

biotechnology The use of techniques to manipulate the genetics of organisms or parts of organisms to produce improved plant varieties, microorganisms, pesticides and other products.

bloom A population explosion of algae in a body of water, often as the result of pollution such as runoff from farmlands.

carcinogen A substance that causes cancer.

chlorination The addition of chlorine to drinking water, sewage and industrial wastes to disinfect the material or to oxidize undesirable compounds.

conservation Measures taken to protect and improve soil and other natural resources.

conservation tillage Any of several methods of cultivation that limit erosion, improve soil quality, increase water infiltration and reduce evaporation.

contour plowing Plowing horizontally around a hill, rather than up and down, in order to limit soil erosion.

crop rotation   A farming method in which different crops are planted in succession on the same field. For example, soil-renewing soybeans may be alternated with corn, which depletes the soil of nutrients.

desalination   The removal of salt from seawater. Also called desalinization.

desertification   The spread of desertlike conditions in arid and semiarid regions.

domestication   The rearing or cultivation of organisms for use by humans.

drought   A prolonged period of dry weather.

erosion   The wearing away of soil by wind or water.

fallow field   A field that is left unplanted during the growing season.

famine   An extreme shortage of food, causing widespread hunger and possibly mass starvation.

feedlot   A relatively small, confined area for raising cattle.

fertile soil   Soil that is rich in the nutrients needed for abundant plant growth.

fertilizer   Nutrients added to the soil to improve plant growth.

fodder crop   A crop raised to provide food for cattle or other domesticated animals.

food chain   A series of organisms in an ecosystem. Each organism feeds on the previous organism in the chain; the initial organism in the chain is a green plant.

gene   The basic unit of heredity. A structure within a cell that determines a hereditary trait, such as leaf shape, disease resistance or milk production.

genetic diversity   The range of genes and, therefore, inheritable information, contained in organisms. The greater the number of species and varieties, the greater the genetic diversity.

genetic engineering   The process of inserting new genetic information into existing cells to modify the characteristics of an organism.

Green Revolution   The dramatic increase in grain production in some developing countries during the 1960s and 1970s, largely as a result of the development of new high-yield varieties.

groundwater   Water contained in pores and cracks of the soil and rocks beneath the Earth's surface. Groundwater fills aquifers and supplies wells and springs.

habitat   The place or region where an organism naturally lives.

heavy metals   Metallic elements such as mercury, lead and arsenic. Even at low concentrations, they can harm organisms, and they tend to accumulate in food chains.

humus   Decomposed organic material in the soil.

integrated pest management   The use of a mixture of methods to control pests, with use of chemical pesticides kept to a minimum.

irrigation   The artificial application of water to farmland.

leaching   The process by which water seeping through soil dissolves and carries away nutrients, pesticides and other materials.

legume   A family of plants, including beans and peas, that obtains usable nitrogen from bacteria that form nodules on the plants' roots.

monoculture   The repeated cultivation of only one kind of crop on a given piece of land.

nitrogen fixing   A biological process by which certain soil bacteria change nitrogen in the air into compounds essential for plant growth.

nutrient   A substance essential for growth and good health.

pesticide   A substance used to control undesirable insects and other pests.

pollutant   Anything introduced into the environment that harms the environment or living organisms.

productivity   In farming, the amount of food produced per unit of land or per animal.

recycling   The process of using something over and over again or of converting discarded materials into new products.

runoff   Rain and other water that runs off the land into lakes, rivers and other bodies of water.

salinization   The buildup of salt in soil, frequently as a result of irrigation.

siltation   The buildup of sediment in reservoirs.

staple   A crop, such as wheat or rice, that is a person's primary source of carbohydrates.

sustainable agriculture   The wise use of land so that the land is as productive in the future as it is at present.

terracing   Plowing sloped land in level steps to limit erosion.

till   To plow. Plowing, or tillage, breaks up or loosens the soil before crops are sown.

topsoil   The uppermost and most fertile layer of soil.

wastewater   Water carrying dissolved or suspended solids from homes, farms, businesses and industries.

wastewater treatment plant   A facility that removes contaminants from wastewater.

watershed   The land area that drains into a stream.

water supply system   A system that collects, treats, stores and distributes drinkable water.

water table   The level in the ground below which the soil is saturated with water.

wetlands   Swamps, marshes, estuaries and other areas that are regularly saturated by water, and whose vegetation is adapted for life in saturated soil conditions.

windbreak   A row of trees or bushes planted at the end of a field to limit wind erosion.

FURTHER READING

Aaseng, Nathan. *Overpopulation: Crisis or Challenge?* New York: Franklin Watts, 1991.

Carothers, Steven W., and Bryan T. Brown. *The Colorado River Through Grand Canyon: Natural History and Human Change.* Tucson: University of Arizona Press, 1991.

Citizen's Guide to Ground-Water Protection. Washington, DC: U.S. Environmental Protection Agency, April 1990.

Elkington, John, et al. *The Green Consumer.* New York: Penguin, 1990.

Farris, John. *The Dust Bowl.* San Diego: Lucent Books, 1989.

Fowler, Cary, and Pat Mooney. *Shattering: Food, Politics, and the Loss of Genetic Diversity.* Tucson: University of Arizona Press, 1990.

Hollender, Jeffrey A. *How to Make the World a Better Place: A Guide to Doing Good.* New York: William Morrow, 1990.

Jorgensen, Eric P. (ed). *The Poisoned Well: New Strategies for Groundwater Protection.* Washington, DC: Island Press, 1989.

Kahn, E.J., Jr. *The Staffs of Life.* Boston: Little, Brown, 1984.

Lappe, Frances Moore. *Diet for a Small Planet* (revised ed). New York: Ballentine Books, 1982.

Lee, Sally. *Pesticides.* New York: Franklin Watts, 1991.

MacKenzie, James J., and Mohamed T. El-Ashry. *Ill Winds: Airborne Pollution's Toll on Trees and Crops.* Washington, DC: World Resources Institute, 1988.

McNeely, Jeffrey A., et al. *Conserving the World's Biological Diversity.* Washington, DC: World Resources Institute, 1990.

Reisner, Marc, and Sarah Bates. *Overtapped Oasis: Reform or Revolution for Western Water.* Washington, DC: Island Press, 1990.

Steinbeck, John. *The Grapes of Wrath.* New York: Viking, 1939.

Stewart, John Cary. *Drinking Water Hazards: How to Know If There Are Toxic Chemicals in Your Water and What to Do If There Are.* Hiram (Ohio): Envirographics, 1990.

Wilson, E.O. (ed). *Biodiversity.* Washington, DC: National Academy Press, 1988.

Periodicals that regularly cover issues associated with food and water supplies:

Environment. Heldreff Publications, 400 Albemarle Street, NW, Washington, DC 20016.

EPA Journal. U.S. Environmental Protection Agency. Superintendent of Documents, GPO, Washington, DC 20402.

Greenpeace. Greenpeace USA, 1436 U Street, NW, Washington, DC 20009.

Science News. Science Service, 1719 N Street, NW, Washington, DC 20036.

Soil and Water Conservation News. Soil Conservation Service, U.S. Department of Agriculture. Superintendent of Documents, GPO, Washington, DC 20402.

Source. United Nations Development Programme, One UN Plaza, New York, NY 10017.

Directories of government agencies and private organizations concerned with environmental issues:

Conservation Directory. National Wildlife Federation, 8925 Leesburg Pike, Vienna, VA 22184.

Directory of Environmental Organizations. Educational Communications, Box 35473, Los Angeles, CA 90035.

Directory of National Environmental Organizations. U.S. Environmental Directories, Box 65156, St. Paul, MN 55165.

INDEX

Photo Credits

Page 4, ©David Carmack/Stock, Boston, Inc.; p. 14, ©Steve Maines/Stock, Boston, Inc.; p. 23, ©Jerry Howard/Stock, Boston, Inc.; p. 25, USDA Photo; p. 36, ©Larry Lefever/Grant Heilman Photography; p. 44, USDA Photo; p. 52, ©Read R. Bruger/The Picture Cube; p. 62, USDA Photo; p. 76, USDA Photo; p. 86, ©Lawrence Migdale/Photo Researchers, Inc.; p. 94, USDA Photo; p. 99, ©Jeffrey Dunn/Stock, Boston, Inc.

Cover, portfolio opener/Problems, ©Terry Eiler/Stock, Boston, Inc.; portfolio page 2, USDA Photo; portfolio page 3, ©Runk/Shoenberger/Grant Heilman Photography; portfolio pages 4–5, ©Grant Heilman/Grant Heilman Photography; portfolio page 6, ©Dagmar Fabricius/Stock, Boston, Inc, Inc; portfolio page 7, ©Daniel Brody/Stock, Boston, Inc.; portfolio page 8, ©Earl Roberge/photo Researchers, Inc.
Portfolio Solutions: Opener, ©Linc Cornell/Stock, Boston, Inc.; portfolio page 2, upper left, ©Grant Heilman/Grant Heilman Photography; portfolio pages 2–3, ©David Austen/Stock, Boston, Inc.; portfolio page 4, ©Marty Heitner/The Picture Cube; portfolio page 5, ©Grant Heilman/Grant Heilman Photography; portfolio page 6–7, ©Allen Green/Photo Researcher, Inc.; portfolio page 8, ©Lawrence Migdale/Stock, Boston, Inc

Art on pages 30–31, 39, 41, 70, 73, 82–83, Wendy Axel; pages 59, 71, 74, Sonja Glassman.

Photo Research by **Inge King.**